# BEYOND CYNICISM

## Towards Ethics in Leadership

# BEYOND CYNICISM

## Towards Ethics in Leadership

---

## The Sheldon M. Chumir Foundation
## for
## Ethics in Leadership

Edited by Marsha P. Hanen
Alex Barber and Jess Hadley

Copyright © 2001 The Sheldon M. Chumir Ethics Foundation

Paperback ISBN 0-9730197-0-0 (acid free paper)




**National Library of Canada Cataloguing in Publication Data**

Main entry under title:

Beyond cynicism


Papers from a symposium held in Calgary.
ISBN 0-9730197-0-0

1. Political ethics—Congresses. 2. Mass media—Moral and ethical
aspects—Congresses. I. Hanen, Marsha P., 1936- II. Barber, Alex.
III. Hadley, Jess. IV. Sheldon M Chumir Foundation for Ethics in
Leadership.
JA79.B49 2001              172              C2001-911741-8




Cover design by Sharon Abra Hanen and David Cassels

Printed at Morriss Printing, Victoria BC, Canada

In memory of Sheldon M. Chumir

1940 – 1992

Scholar, Humanitarian, Legislator

# CONTENTS

# ACKNOWLEDGEMENTS

---

This book grew out of the first public symposium held on the weekend of December 2-3, 2000, by the Sheldon M. Chumir Foundation for Ethics in Leadership. The symposium was held to inaugurate the Foundation's programs and to celebrate the legacy of Sheldon Chumir on what would have been his 60th birthday. From the outset, the Foundation had undertaken to publish the symposium proceedings, and the papers were posted on our web site as they became available. We are pleased now, on the first anniversary of the symposium, to be fulfilling our original commitment by publishing the proceedings, together with an Afterword, in book form.

Naturally, our first debt of gratitude goes to the symposium participants whose work is represented here: Alan Borovoy, Tom Flanagan, Kathleen Mahoney, Maureen Maloney, Peter Desbarats and Bob Rae. Each of them responded with unfailing enthusiasm and generosity to our invitation to participate in our celebration weekend, and to engage with the audience in meaningful discussion of the topics at hand. Lindsay Gluck, the Foundation's 2000-2001 Intern, has kindly consented to the publication of her research paper as the concluding essay in the volume. Her topic arose from our many discussions about cynicism in connection with public life, and seems an appropriate continuation of the debate surrounding some of the issues raised during the symposium. Sydney Sharpe provided reflections on ethics in government during the symposium, and Janet Keeping, Sheilah Martin and David Taras kindly agreed to chair sessions, which they did most ably.

The symposium itself, and especially the participation of a number of students, was made possible by several sponsors: Bennett Jones Barristers and Solicitors, The Kahanoff Foundation, Enbridge Inc., Petro-Canada and RBC Dominion Securities. We offer our thanks to each of these organizations, and to *The Calgary Herald* for media sponsorship. We are also most grateful to the weekend celebration committee, co-chaired by Stephanie Felesky, The Honourable Ron Ghitter, Q.C. (who also chaired the celebration dinner), and Senator Dan Hays; and to the hard-working dinner committee (Judge Gary Cioni, Aron Eichler, Sheila Harris, Brian Heffernan, Greg Horton, Julie Johnston, John Scott, Steve Sparks and Frances Wright), co-chaired by Darryl Raymaker, Q.C. and Michèle Stanners, all of whom helped to make the weekend such a success. Aron Eichler video-taped the dinner proceedings, from which we transcribed Bob Rae's presentation. And we were immeasurably helped by Foundation staff and volunteers Sharon Hanen, Jeff Robillard, Ingrid Salyn, Melissa Trono, Linda Van Dyke and, especially, Lindsay Gluck and Elaine Wojtkiw, whose organizational skills made the planning and execution of the event proceed with minimum chaos and maximum good cheer.

In the preparation of the manuscript for publication,

we have been blessed by the capable editing skills of Alex Barber and Jess Hadley, who have, with great patience, worked through the presentations, attempting to preserve the immediacy of the symposium presentations while ensuring that the resulting volume would also be reader friendly. Ingrid Salyn transcribed from tapes those papers we did not have in written form; and David Cassels has put the entire manuscript together, with careful attention to form and detail. His technical and design skills are evident not only in the layout of the book itself, but in the execution of Sharon Abra Hanen's striking cover design.

Keijo Isomaa of Morriss Printing has been most generous in working through the details of publication with us and seeing to the printing of the volume. The photograph of Sheldon Chumir on the back cover was taken by Brian Harder; photos on the front cover are by Clayton B. Kaplar, with the exception of Peter Desbarats' which is by Sheila Harris.

Finally, I want to express my personal appreciation to the Foundation's Board, Joel Bell, Betty Flagler, Ron Ghitter, Cliff O'Brien and Aritha Van Herk for their unfailing support of the publication project and the symposium from which it resulted.


Marsha P. Hanen, President
The Sheldon M. Chumir Foundation for Ethics in Leadership
December, 2001

# PREFACE

---

Sheldon Chumir was, by anyone's standards, an outstanding human being. Born in Calgary on December 3rd, 1940, he excelled at virtually every endeavour he undertook. As a Rhodes scholar, tax lawyer, rock concert promoter, politician, civil libertarian, public interest advocate, hockey player, businessman and many other things, Sheldon worked and played with passionate intensity. His life was characterized by intelligence, humour, hard work, decency, and fairness. As a student, Sheldon achieved excellence in sports, academic pursuits, and student activities. After completing a law degree at the University of Alberta as his class's gold medallist in 1963, Sheldon was awarded a Rhodes scholarship to study at Oxford. When he returned to Canada in 1965 he pursued careers in the law, business and politics.

These accomplishments were impressive, but Sheldon wished to help those whose civil rights had been infringed and so he left his practice as a tax lawyer in 1976 and set up his own firm to defend the rights of the powerless. His commitment to civil liberties was unmatched; typically, he worked *pro bono* for causes that he felt were important. He also taught civil liberties at the University of Calgary Law School.

Sheldon loved to debate issues, recognizing that principled and respectful disagreement was vital to the democratic process. His approach to issues was characterized by careful reflection and independence of mind. His educational and legal experiences turned him into a vigorous supporter of public education, civil rights and individual freedoms. Whatever the issue, Sheldon could always be found acting for the underdog – for the person or group he felt needed his help.

As a politician Sheldon was convinced that voters wanted political leaders to strive for fairness and honesty in all of their dealings. He rejected the notion that politics was a blood sport where only the ruthless could survive. His political instincts helped him to get elected in 1986 – the first Liberal elected in Calgary in over fifteen years – as a Member of Alberta's Legislative Assembly for the riding of Calgary-Buffalo. On being elected, an elated Sheldon proclaimed: "The electors of Calgary Buffalo are a diverse group that have shown great collective wisdom, independence and a sense of adventure in their selection of an MLA. What can you say about electors who choose a Jewish civil libertarian bachelor with a beard and fluffy hair?" He was re-elected in 1989.

In addition to his unique personality, Sheldon also had a unique perspective in that he was familiar with the internal dynamics of both the public and private sectors. He was, therefore, able to conceptualize and to criticize the strengths and weaknesses of both systems.

Sheldon sensed that our society suffers from a crisis of leadership. Both in government and in business, he perceived that people had lost faith in the capacity of established institutions to meet the needs of those they served. The first sign of this loss of faith was the public's increasing reluctance to spend time reflecting on issues relating to the public good.

When he died at the age of just fifty-one in January of 1992 following a brief illness, there was an enormous outpouring of respect and admiration not only from his many friends, but from people from all walks of life who felt how keenly they would miss his integrity, his dedication to humanitarian causes, his gentle humour and sense of fun, and his genuine warmth toward people from every corner of the community. Following his death, Sheldon was recognized by the Law Society of Alberta and posthumously awarded the Distinguished Service Award for Service to the Community. The inscription on the award reads in part:

> Founder of the Alberta Civil Liberties Association, he was a tireless champion in *pro bono* work for various unpopular causes and wrongs to be set right. His spirit lives on through the Sheldon Chumir Foundation for Ethics in Leadership, created as his last wish as a legacy for Canada.

He dedicated the bulk of his estate to the creation of the Sheldon M. Chumir Foundation for Ethics in Leadership. In so doing, he said:

> I have sensed for many years that our society suffers from a crisis of leadership at all levels of government and in community and business organizations. I believe that an ethical want underlies and contributes to this

crisis... I have witnessed how leadership exercised by individuals motivated by high ethical purpose can bring about significant change for the betterment of our society. My desire is that the Foundation advance and encourage this type of leadership in our community...[and that it] operate so as to influence ethical actions in the practical world of politics, business, government and community structures and processes.

Arising directly from Sheldon's own convictions, the Foundation's mission is to promote principled, ethically motivated action by individuals and organizations – action which is community-minded in the sense that it attends to the impact of decisions and actions on those who are affected by them. It seeks to advance this purpose by engaging in and encouraging ethical education of current and prospective leaders and fostering awareness and informed discussion of issues in the public realm that have an ethical dimension.

Sheldon believed that if political and business leaders were better informed about the ethical implications of their decisions, society would be greatly improved. To work toward this, the Foundation offers two annual fellowships for professionals in media and public affairs that provide skilled individuals with time to conduct a non-partisan investigation of a particular issue related to ethics in the public realm, and to disseminate the work widely. The Foundation has also created annual internships to allow one or more graduate students or recent graduates to carry out research and participate in community outreach programs supporting ethics in leadership. The Foundation produces a periodic newsletter, and comments on ethical issues of public importance. It also enters into partnerships with other organizations to support education on ethics in public life and has initiated a series of public forums and symposia in which leaders and prospective leaders engage with the general public on national and international issues relating to ethics.

This volume, commemorating Sheldon's 60<sup>th</sup> birthday and building on his legacy, collects four presentations from the Foundation's first annual symposium, entitled *Beyond Cynicism* and concludes with an essay by the Foundation's first intern. Although the individual papers have been available on the Foundation's web site, there were a number of requests to have them collected into one volume. The book will be made available to school and university libraries and to other organizations with an interest in these issues. Although much in public life has changed in the past year, in many ways comments on ethics and civil liberties are even more pertinent now than they were a year ago.

# INTRODUCTION

---

**Cynic.**       *One disposed to deny and sneer at the sincerity or goodness of human motives and actions.*

**Pessimist.**  *One who habitually takes the worst view of things.*

**Skeptic.**     *One who maintains a doubting attitude with reference to some particular question or statement.*

*– Oxford English Dictionary*

You will recall December of the year 2000. In the United States, after weeks of ballot counting and legal wrangling, the closest presidential election in American history had yet to be decided. Canada's highly partisan federal election, on the other hand, had just concluded with a record low voter turnout. Cynicism and pessimism relating to their respective leaders and the conduct of public life was common in both Canada and the United States, as it had been for a number of years.  It was during this tumultuous political period that the Sheldon Chumir Foundation for Ethics in Leadership convened its inaugural symposium in Calgary.  The event coincided with what would have been Sheldon's 60th birthday.

The theme of the weekend celebration, *Beyond Cynicism: Towards Ethics in Leadership*, was not only timely, but very much in keeping with the way Sheldon thought politics ought to be.  As a political leader, Sheldon was concerned that the public perceived a gap between their expectations as citizens and the actions and ethics of their representatives.  This ethical disconnection, according to Sheldon, has had dire consequences for democracy.  In the last twenty years the public has gone beyond an attitude of informed skepticism, which can generate a positive approach to the possibilities for citizen engagement and a focus on community values as a basis for decisions and actions in the public realm.  Instead, we have become less willing than before to join political parties, to engage in electoral politics, to participate in community minded activities, and to reflect on the public good.  Cynical attitudes towards politics and politicians seem to have become the norm; but cynicism is ultimately self-defeating, leading to a kind of passivity in relation to public life.  One of the very real dangers here is that in a democracy persuasive argument is a major way in which political leaders can bring public support to bear on issues, and if the public no longer trusts what their leaders are saying, the ability to lead is seriously eroded.

What is to be done about this?  Who bears the responsibility for halting our drift toward cynicism and political despair?  Can our attitudes toward politics and public life be changed?  How can we ensure that decisions and actions in the public realm are for the public good?  What responsibilities do the media have towards democracy?

Do advancements in technology help or hurt the democratic process? These were some of the questions that a panel of outstanding speakers attempted to address during the Chumir Foundation's inaugural symposium.

The symposium began with a talk by Alan Borovoy of the Canadian Civil Liberties Association. Borovoy, like Sheldon Chumir, has had a lifelong interest in the protection of civil liberties. In his address, entitled *Keeping God in His Place: Protecting Religion from Society and Protecting Society from Religion*, Borovoy outlined his concern with the views that have been associated with Canadian Alliance leader Stockwell Day. Specifically, Borovoy questioned whether the religious fundamentalist worldview was compatible with the type of public policy necessary for extremely diverse and, for the most part, secular societies.

Borovoy argued that fundamentalism, or the tendency to view the 'Will of God' as paramount in decisions concerning public policy, was injurious to democracy and civil liberties. In the give and take of political debate and discussion, it tends to range mere mortals on one side of the debate and the deity on the other. Moreover, the 'Will of God' is often described as a 'mystery' to which the laws of rational discussion do not always apply, making reasoned discourse more difficult. According to Borovoy, equally dangerous are government forays into the realm of religious freedoms. Where, in areas such as education and the media, does one draw the line between church and state? At the conclusion of his talk, Professors Tom Flanagan and Kathleen Mahoney, both of the University of Calgary, contributed their comments from their two quite different perspectives. Their remarks highlight the wide spectrum of views on the subject of the role of religion in a society characterized by increasing diversity, and emphasize both some of the significant differences in point of view and the potential for agreement on a number of issues.

On the second day of the symposium, Maureen Maloney, Professor of Law and co-director of the Institute for Conflict Resolution at the University of Victoria, gave a presentation entitled *Ethics, Leadership, and Government*. In her remarks, Maloney questioned to what extent we can claim to have a consensus for what constitutes ethical conduct and noted that, of late, the relationship between citizens and their governments has been changing. What is it, she asked, that makes ethical behavior of such importance in public officials? Rapid economic and technological advances have produced significant changes that, according to Maloney, mean that rules for ethical conduct must constantly be reformulated. For example, the 'virtual reality' world of the Internet raises new problems relating to 'privacy' and 'truthfulness'. The ethical conduct we expect in the future will likely be very different from the type of conduct that we expected in the past; but Professor Maloney was able to offer a number of principles that, she believed, needed to inform our approach to ethics in government.

Later that day Peter Desbarats, who holds the Maclean Hunter Chair of Communications Ethics at Ryerson Polytechnic University, gave an address entitled *Media Ethics in the Age of Multimedia – the Real Meaning of Convergence*. Desbarats commented on the ways in which technological innovation and corporate media mergers are affecting media ethics. Have we reached a point, he asked, where 'ethical journalism' is a contradiction in terms? The result of these trends, according to Desbarats, is worrisome. In particular, he lamented the fact that media concentration is now regarded as inevitable and suggested that as the Internet has become more important, increasing the speed with which news is being presented to the public, the most important feature of good journalism – its creative, artistic aspect — has suffered. But he also saw hopeful signs of broader involvement in journalistic enterprises arising from the ever-increasing use of the Internet.

The weekend concluded with a talk by the Honourable Bob Rae, former Premier of Ontario. His address, *In Defense of Politics*, reviewed current trends in Canadian and American politics, and challenged the notion that politics is at its root a dirty business incapable of meeting ethical standards. According to Rae, politics is inevitable in all of our relationships, not just those relating to our governments. He argued that politics is about power in all its forms, and that those with the courage to stand up publicly for their beliefs are not always popular but that one's beliefs can be presented for discussion without an accompanying personal disparagement of one's opponent. The political process is a necessary undertaking and, although citizen views may differ, this should not dissuade us from seeking consensus through respectful dialogue.

This book also includes, as an 'Afterword', the research project prepared by the Foundation's first intern, Lindsay Gluck. Her work attempts to analyze and explain how and why different generations view politics differently. In helping to organize the symposium, she became interested in some of the problems surrounding cynicism and disengagement and, in her paper, she examines economic, political, and social changes in an attempt to explain why many young people feel alienated from the political process. Her findings, while disheartening in some respects, provide a necessary assessment of the status quo, which she hopes can serve as a precursor to positive change.

All of the issues and concerns that our symposium speakers raised continue to be debated and analyzed and we hope that this volume will provide both information and motivation to continue that debate. As Sheldon Chumir so often commented, it is through thoughtful, lively and respectful discussion of disagreements that societies move ahead.

## · 1 ·
## Alan Borovoy

# KEEPING GOD IN HIS PLACE:
## Protecting Religion From Society
## and
## Protecting Society From Religion[1]

The rise of Stockwell Day to national prominence has impelled all of us to examine, yet again, the difficult questions of the relationship between religious practices and secular politics. In the past few months, we have been engulfed in an ocean of polemics on the subject. On the one hand, we have critics saying that anyone who believes in "fairy tales", such as creationism, can't be trusted with governmental power. On the other side, defenders have countered that no other politicians are subjected to such scrutiny about *their* religious beliefs. Critics have expressed the fear that fundementalists with power would try to impose their beliefs on the rest of us. To which the defenders respond that they would do no such thing, but in any event we are all entitled to be *influenced* by our respective religious beliefs.

In my view, religious fundamentalists – no less than religious moderates and secular humanists – are, of

1. This chapter is prepared, with only minor editing, from the symposium tapes.

course, entitled to be influenced by the things they believe in. Moreover, my worldview, my conception of pluralistic society is such that people are entitled to draw comfort from any "fairy tales" they like. That's really none of my business.

But there are problems when we see some people approach secular society from a religious vantage point. And as I reflected about this problem, I identified at least what seems to me to be the difficulty. A number of religious fundamentalists, when they have approached secular politics, have attempted, when they tried to resolve public policy disputes, to invoke "authorities" which cannot be challenged or questioned. They have said to us effectively: "we want you to implement the Will of God, as we see it."

In the case of Stockwell Day himself, it is reported that a number of years ago, in the context of some dispute at the religious school he administered there was some question as to whether the curriculum conformed to legal requirements. His reported response at the time, at least in part, was that the curriculum there is not set by the government; it is set, among others, by God. Now how is a mere mortal supposed to argue with that? And, you see by the act of invoking authority of that kind, he removes the question from human controversy. And, a few years later it is reported that when a number of gay leaders were received at the Alberta Legislature, he described the event as an "offence against God".

In truth, he is only the latest of this phenomenon. We have experienced the same thing from others. In the past 15 years or so we have had the Christian Heritage Party. In fact I brought one of their quotes with me – I can't commit these things to memory. Responding to the Supreme Court decision which awarded spousal benefits to gay people they said if the word "supremacy" has any meaning at all, it means that God's revealed condemnation of homosexual unions must be respected in all Canadian legislation and judicial rulings. And on the subject of pornography their position is described, as saying that deliberate immodesty for the purpose of sexual stimulation is an offense against humankind and God. The answer: tighter censorship.

And, of course, on the question of abortion they have weighed in similarly as has the Evangelical Fellowship, as have the more mainstream bodies like the Catholic Bishops Conference and even some MP's who have talked quite openly and attempted to persuade the rest of us to accept the notion that the fetus, in the eyes of God, is every bit as worthy of protection as are others. It is in the eyes of God that this is supposed to become ultimately persuasive. Now to be fair, and before my brother Flanagan[2] sets upon me for what I have said so far, to be fair, this kind of thing has emanated not only from the religious right but also from the religious left. And I brought with me one of their quotes. This is from the mainstream churches during the height of the Cold War. They said: "We can conceive of no circumstances under which the use of nuclear weapons could be consistent with the Will of God and we must therefore conclude that nuclear weapons must also be rejected as a means or threat of deterrent." And they went on to quote favorably an American clergyman who said: "It is a sin, not merely to use or to threaten to use but merely to build and to possess nuclear weapons."

Well at the base of it all is this claim of mere mortals to *know* the Will of God. Now it is my view that mere mortals, when they attempt to discern the Will of God, find themselves in a hopeless dilemma. Any command or commandment or policy direction emanating from the Almighty is immediately beyond question or challenge. How can mere human beings challenge what comes from perfection? But the difficulty is that at the same time we know that we are fallible human beings who might be wrong. It also

2. Reference here is to Tom Flanagan, Professor of Political Science, University of Calgary, and commentator at the symposium.

then means that we might be wrong about the things we believe in. So we must question what we believe in. We must always question it. Then, the moment we acknowledge that we must question these things we are no longer treating them as emanating from God. They can't be both subject to question and immune from question at one and the same time. You can't do it.

Moreover, how is a mere mortal supposed to recognize God in the event of a communication or revelation? There are no logical axioms, no scientific principles by which we can do it. We have to rely on our subjective, limited, finite, intuitive capacity. How can we rely on them to be the judge of matters so enormous? And, I have often worried that humans couldn't recognize an absolute if they fell over one. And this applies not only to the people in this century but also to the peoples from antiquity whose claims to have had divine encounters are relied upon by some of the people I am criticizing.

Take my favorite case – the case of the Bible's Abraham. When he got the command to kill his only son Isaac, how did he know that was God? How did he know that was the voice of God he was hearing? Wasn't it just as plausible to attribute that to the Devil? Or to his own imagination? Why not? Well the answer we get from a lot of people is "Faith". But that is an awfully elusive reply. Faith in whom and in what? In order for Abraham to obey an awful command like that, at the very least he had to have faith in himself. He had to believe in his own ability to identify the contents and the source of that terrible command.

And what do we say about all of the people in contemporary society? We hear from time to time of terrible crimes committed by people who claim that they were ordered to do so by God. How do we deny those claims? Morality? We say God wouldn't command people to do things like that. How do we tie God to our concepts of right and wrong? We're supposed to get our morality from God – not the other way around.

So there are simply no criteria, and in fact taking it one step further, couldn't God behave in ways we in our limited, finite ways might think of as inconsistent without telling us the reasons? In His all-knowing reasoning, His all-knowing perfect wisdom, He could have good reasons to withhold the reasons from us. So how can we do it? Now I hasten to point out this is not to denigrate the role, the important role, that [the] world's great religions have played over the years. This is to register not a word on whether there is or is not a God. It simply says that in a pluralistic society of colliding values, we cannot presume to divine the Divine Will without reposing absolutist faith either in our own powers of discernment or in some other finite human recipient of a claimed revelation.

There's another problem with invoking the Divine Will and that is that it neglects what one of my favorite philosophers used to call "the tragic sense of life". The fact is that so many of our public policy disputes are not conflicts between good and evil. They are conflicts between good and good and right and right. If we want more money for health care, we might have to have less money for housing. We can't have it all. We have to choose. They are all virtues. How does the Divine Will help us choose which is more virtuous and in which situations?

Let me go back to two of the earlier examples. First, pornography, and on the other side of the equation is democracy's belief in freedom of expression – no small matter. Now so many of the religious people tell us that democracy and law owe a lot to their religious tradition. But how do we write a law so precise that it will get the awful stuff, that the Christian Heritage Foundation is talking about, without catching in the same net a lot of other material – perhaps artistic expression and valid artistic expression? We've seen time and again that these laws invariably overshoot the mark. So how can we write a law that precise? And, we always have to ask, is it worth the risk? I'm not trying to resolve the question now. I'm simply posing the question – simply raising it because it can't be resolved just by invoking the Will of God. You might indeed find the Will of God on both sides, not simply on one side.

And, on nuclear weapons, those church leaders made those remarks at the height of the Cold War, when we faced the threat, the malevolent threat of nuclear weapons, from the Soviet Union that already had overwhelming conventional superiority to us. Now, in that situation, should we have divested ourselves of nuclear weapons? Remember those religious people who said that it's a sin to even possess them. Should we then have renounced them? And with what result? Those same religious people, I'm sure, believe in the survival of democracy. How do they square their belief in the survival of democracy with their claim about nuclear weapons: that it's a sin even to possess them? Again, I'm not trying here to resolve nuclear strategy – simply to pose the question, suggesting that invoking the Will of God is not very helpful for these purposes.

As regards the relationship between religious belief and secular society, there is yet another cluster of issues to be faced. On this score, I believe that Canadian society should do less to promote – and more to protect – religious belief. There are at least two ways in which Canadian society is improperly promoting religious belief – by mandating religious exercises and instruction in the public schools and by extending financial assistance to the religious schools.

At the moment, it appears that public school boards in a number of provinces may prescribe religious instruction and exercises for their students. While I believe that it is ethically permissible for the government and the public schools to promote *knowledge about* various religions, I believe it is ethically impermissible for them to promote a *belief in* any particular religion, and I also consider it ethically impermissible for them to engage students in the ritual exercises belonging to any religious faith such as, for example, the Lord's Prayer.

Since youngsters from all religious faiths are required by law to attend school, their parents' religious freedom is infringed to the extent that such youngsters are subjected to official pressures to receive instruction and join in exercises at variance with the beliefs taught at home. And, to the extent that the state officially favours a religion other than what is observed in the home, the parents' religious equality is infringed. It is no answer to provide, as most jurisdictions do, a right of exemption from such instruction and exercises. Conspicuous withdrawal from the classroom on religious grounds is often experienced as an unpleasant disability associated with religious dissent. This too is incompatible with a genuine freedom and with religious equality.

I am similarly troubled by the growing pressures in this country for governments to provide religious day schools with significant amounts of public tax money. Any government funding of religious schools beyond what is already constitutionally required would mean that virtually *all* religious schools would be entitled to comparable treatment. In such circumstances, it is reasonable to expect a growing exodus from the public school system. At some point, there is a good chance that even mainstream Protestants would be enticed to open their own schools. A country in which so many youngsters attended religious schools could well be a much different place from what it is today. For all their faults, the public schools provide the community with a unique opportunity to promote inter-group cooperation and respect. To whatever extent this institution became significantly weakened, there would be a commensurate weakening of our society's ability to address incipient inter-group tensions.

My final remarks – I go from the situation where we are improperly promoting religious belief to the situation where we are inadequately protecting religious belief. In fact, there are some situations in which governments have adopted measures imposing affirmative restrictions on certain religious expression. I have three examples.

First, the British Columbia Bubble Zone legislation. In British Columbia a few years ago a statute was enacted prohibiting people from expressing disapproval of abortion within fifty meters of a great many abortion clinics. In short, they say you can't picket within half a football field of these abortion clinics. Now it's one thing to protect doctors and patients from physical intimidation but it's another thing entirely to protect them from social disapproval. Now I know some people say they can always express their views somewhere else. This reminds me much of a comment I made (I love quoting myself) a number of years ago in a different context. I said, "in Canada we don't ban demonstrations, we reroute them." And that is the sort of problem that we have here.

Currently the Saskatchewan Human Rights Commission is in proceedings against the *Saskatoon Star-Phoenix* and a self-styled Christian fundamentalist who had placed an ad in that newspaper. The ad showed a diagonal line drawn through the image of two men holding hands. To be sure, a repugnant ad. Nor was it redeemed by the inclusion of biblical citations. If the newspaper had rejected it, I would have applauded. Illegality is another story.

The Saskatchewan Commission argued that barring the ad would interfere minimally with the fundamentalist's freedom of religious expression. According to the commission, he was still free to read his Bible, donate money, talk to his fellow believers, and distribute Bibles. But, in order to have their views even considered, activists must often employ attention-getting measures. To confine proselytizers to polite discussion is to replace freedom of communication with freedom of soliloquy.

Although the Ontario Human Rights Code has no such anti-hate provision, the Ontario Commission has nevertheless been following suit. This Commission is now acting against a printer who had refused to print the stationery of a gay and lesbian organization. As a "born-again Christian", the printer insisted that he conscientiously objected to this job. While I share the Commission's disdain for this printer's views about homosexuality, I believe that his position should be defended. I think human rights commissions properly go after people. People who operate businesses on the public market should be required to serve gay people but not gay causes. If this had been a gay dentist and they came to him and said: "No, I won't print anything for a gay person" we should go after him, but as to a gay organization and its ideology, he should be protected from serving it.

Well, we can make all kinds of distinctions. In our pluralistic democracy it is important to protect the integrity of religious belief from an intrusive, secular politics and it is important to protect the integrity of secular politics from a sanctimonious religious belief.

Whether we are fans or foes of Stockwell Day, we are in his debt for making us think through these problems yet one more time, no, yet several more times. This debate, I suspect, will go on in perpetuity. At least, I hope it goes on in perpetuity. All of which is as always, your honour, your eminence, your worship, respectfully submitted. Thank you.

## **COMMENTARIES**

*Thomas Flanagan,*
*Professor of Political Science, University of Calgary*

I should emphasize at the beginning that I largely agree with Alan Borovoy. I like to say that because I think that it is probably profoundly embarrassing to him to realize how much we agree upon. So I would like to emphasize that. But there are inevitably a few points on which I would make additional comments. So I am going to pick out the few things on which I disagree with Alan; and other topics on which I don't say anything, you can assume that I am more or less on side with what he had to say.

First of all, the title of the presentation, which has been adopted for the title of the session – "Keeping God in His Place". I find the title needlessly antagonistic to religious believers. People of deep religious faith don't think that God belongs just in a specific compartment of their lives. They believe that God is present in all they say and do. The problem for politics is to find a modus vivendi that allows people of different faiths, or of no faith, to live together peacefully and cooperatively. Referring to that modus vivendi as "Keeping God in His Place" is not a promising start towards bringing people together. I don't think there is actually anything in Alan's views which are hostile to religion, but I don't know why then one would rhetorically begin by taking an antagonistic title.

Secondly, if you want to quote Stockwell Day you should quote the whole statement. So here's the whole statement as I found it in Claire Hoy's recent biography of Stockwell Day: "God's Law is clear. Standards of education are not set by government, but by God, the Bible, the home and the school." And here my dinosaur[3] gave me some advice and he said if you want these people to know

3. Reference here is to a toy brought by Dr. Flanagan and introduced to the audience at the beginning of his commentary.

what you are saying you have to use a prop.

God, the Bible, the home and the school. If we ask for an interpretation, if we ask for the Education Minister's approval we are recognizing his authority. I think it is important to know exactly what Stock said. Moreover, a sense of context is essential in interpreting his words. When he made this statement in 1984, Mr. Day was appearing before an Alberta Legislative Committee on behalf of a coalition of independent religious schools. The sponsors of some schools were willing to accept government approval and review of their curriculum but others at the time were not. Mr. Day was trying to present both points of view to the committee in an attempt to broker a compromise. It is also important to take note of the situation. Mr. Day was representing people who were seeking to be left alone by government, to conduct the education of their children as they saw fit. Neither they nor he were attempting to impose anything upon anyone outside their own families. In other words, they were not proposing this conception of Divine approval of curriculum as a principle of legislation to be adopted by government and implemented for the community as a whole. They were asking to be allowed to live that way in their own lives.

Now of course there are many vital and hotly contested questions about the limits of parental control over children, but all this is quite different from a theocratic claim to rule on the basis of God's Will. I join with Alan in rejecting the principle of theocracy as an appropriate principle for government, but I don't think that the quotation from Stockwell Day has anything to do with a theocratic claim to rule.

Finally, one should note that those who claim absolute immunity from all government oversight of education lost their struggle with the Alberta government; in fact they lost in the courts. Well Mr. Day went on to become a member of that government illustrating the absence of

theocracy in his own political views. So I agree completely with Alan in his condemnation of the theocratic impulse.
But I think the example of Mr. Day's quotation is not well
chosen to illustrate the argument he wants to make.

The third point – and here he delivered a pre-emp-
tive strike, taking away my criticism – he was right to think
that I would bring up this point. In the notes (it wasn't a full
fledged paper) that I received to read a few days ago, all of
Alan's examples of theocratic intervention in politics come
from the political right.

But, I would say that in Canada, such meddling is
actually more common on the left. Adherents of the social
gospel from J. S. Woodsworth to the Reverend William
Phipps have never been hesitant to deduce specific social
and economic policies from the reading of Holy Writ. The
Canadian Conference of Catholic Bishops did the same
thing in the 1980's when they condemned the market economy. I would note in passing that the man who is reputed
to be the leading candidate for the leadership of the
Saskatchewan NDP is a United Church minister. The history of the NDP and CCF before it is full of United Church
ministers or other denominations who have never been shy
about saying what they think God's Will is for social policy.

Of course Alan is right to point to the Christian
Heritage party and other parties who in their own way are
also theocratic but the scale of the problem is actually, in
my view, quite a bit larger on the left side of the spectrum
than on the right side of the spectrum in Canada. I must
say I don't actually worry very much about people making
statements of that type. I think that there are plenty of
countervailing sources of criticism. And I think it is important to point out the theocratic nature of such statements
whether they come from the right or the left, but I also think
that in a free society people have to be free to make theocratic arguments. I think that Alan would agree with me on
that point. So once again we really are together.

Now we come probably to a major disagreement. I agree that under present conditions public schools in Canada should not teach a particular religious faith or promote the observance of a particular religion, but I think we should regard this as a pragmatic matter of time and place, not as an absolute truth about politics.

At the time of Confederation, when almost everyone in Canada was either Protestant or Roman Catholic and almost everyone thought that education had to have a religious foundation, it was probably quite reasonable to set up separate systems of Protestant and Catholic schools rather than a single system of secular public schools. Today, most Protestants probably favor the secular model while most Catholics still seem to want religious, or at least Catholic schools for themselves. But what about the Protestants, Jews, Muslims and others who want religious rather that secular education for their children? Alan's view seems to be, "okay let them have it if they are able and willing to pay for it." Now that is fine with me as far as it goes. But it takes no account of the fact that these parents are already being heavily taxed to pay for the secularized schools they do not wish to use. For once and perhaps only once I find myself in agreement with the United Nations that Ontario ought to take steps to do what Alberta and Quebec have already done, namely, to provide some financial compensation to parents who find themselves forced, as it were, to pay twice if they want a religious education for their children. I confess to being a little surprised by Alan's insistence on the public model of education. I would have thought that the General Counsel of the Canadian Civil Liberties Association might have remembered the words of John Stuart Mill from one of the greatest books on liberty that anyone has ever written. And I quote:

> A general State education is mere contrivance for moulding people to be exactly like one another: and as the mould in which it casts them is that which pleases the predominant power in the government, whether this be a monarch, a priesthood, an aristocracy or the majority of the existing generation, in proportion as it is efficient and successful, it establishes a despotism over the mind, leading by natural tendency to one over the body. An education established and controlled by the State should only exist, if it exists at all, as one among many competing experiments.

That's from the final chapter of John Stuart Mill's "Essay on Liberty". On this as on many other issues I am happy to take my stand with John Stuart Mill, the spiritual father of modern liberalism.

*Kathleen Mahoney*
*Professor of Law, University of Calgary*

I got to know Sheldon when I first started teaching. He was teaching the human rights course and he handed it to me so we spent quite a bit of time together – him sort of bringing me up to speed on human rights and we had our debates starting then and the torch was passed to me to do the human rights. And then that's when I encountered Alan Borovoy and when he says that these debates go on in perpetuity I certainly know what that means. Alan and I have been at one another now for, I would say, probably twenty years. But it is always a pleasure. I'd also like to say before I begin my commentary on what Alan has said today that this particular topic is very apropos Sheldon – his views, what propelled him into politics in the first place, and also it is quite serendipitous, you might say I think, that this topic has come up at this particular time when for the first time, in as long as I can remember, religion has become an issue in the political context here in Alberta and in Canada in this recent election. So I think it is really quite interesting and I am quite happy to participate in this debate at this time on this particular topic.

I too, like Tom Flanagan, agree with many of the points that Alan has made. I suppose my points of issue come up with things he didn't say. And, I'm going to address some of those. But before I do that I want to underscore, perhaps add a bit to the things he did say.

I think it is important to make the view quite strongly that religious belief is not the issue here at all. As somebody, I think, pointed out during the course of the election, all the leaders of the various parties had a religion, including Mr. Day. And yet none of us, generally speaking, knew what those religions of the other leaders were and yet all of us seemed to know what Mr. Day's religion was. And the question is why were we so aware of that. I think the answer to that is because the religion had spilled over into the public realm during the course of the campaign and before. Because back in the good old days, in the early eighties, was when I first met Sheldon Chumir, he was fighting a battle called "Save Public Education" and I see Sheila Harris is here today and she was his comrade in that struggle and many Calgarians got involved.

On the other side of that fight was Stockwell Day and that's what propelled him into politics as well, if my recollection is correct. So this battle goes back a long way and Mr. Day's opinion in those days was, as has already been stated, that not only should government funding be used to support religious schools but there should be no government regulations on what is taught in religious schools, which of course raises starkly the public policy issue as to what is the government's role in the education of our children. Is there a legitimate role there to say that religion should not drive the curriculum, the government should? And then that brings up the issue, of course, of secularism versus religion, and Mr. Flanagan has spoken about how secularism should just be one view. But I think over history governments have learned, at least in free and democratic societies, that having public policy driven by religion does not usually work very well. And I think we can see that example played out in many areas of the world today. In fact, most of the wars being fought today in the world, are being fought because one side does not agree with the other side's religious beliefs. We only have to look to the Middle East, to Ireland, to Afghanistan, to India, to Tibet and other places in the world where people kill one another, massacre one another, on a regular basis because of differences in religious belief, and the government being driven by, in its policy, the religion of one side or the other. So there are many good reasons why governments and their policies and the schooling of their children must be secular as opposed to taking up any particular religious belief.

In so far as the point of the role of churches, however, in shaping public policy and having their say, I certainly would not oppose, for example, the Council of Catholic Bishops or the World Council of Churches or any other religiously motivated group from commenting on public policy, be that nuclear weapons or be that poverty or hunger. Obviously churches work on the basis of moral principles and they live in societies which are governed by public policy and politicians who often take political views that they disagree with. That, in their religious views, impacts very negatively on the people that they care about. I think there is quite a distinction that needs to be drawn between religious people taking up a view in the Cold War on nuclear arms and politicians saying that nuclear arms should not be used because of religious reasons. I think there is a distinction there that needs to be made and I am not sure that it came through in Alan's remarks but maybe I heard them wrongly. If he intended to say that religious organizations should not comment on public policy, I think he is wrong.

I wanted to make another point too about religion informing public policy and how it impacts on individuals. I think that is very important. I am going to look to more extreme examples because sometimes I think we get a little bit confused when examples are in a country such as Canada where we all enjoy a large amount of freedom in everything that we do. But in many countries of the world, where people don't, I think we can see more starkly the effects of the religiously motivated ideologies on individuals. And I am thinking here of somewhere in the neighborhood of 87 million women in the world today who are subjected to genital mutilation as a part of either religious or cultural practice. I'm also thinking of women who are forced to cover their entire bodies because they are thought to be impure by government fiat and they can only look through a small slit in the covering over their faces. I'm also thinking about the use of violence justified by religion to discipline women who want to work outside the home. I'm thinking of the practice of denying women the right to drive a car for religious reasons. These are very, very severe impacts on individual liberty, particularly of women who are affected by the use of religion all over the world. I think that is a very important criterion to understand how religion is used.

And on the abortion question, of course that is the one that is closest to us in North America in the sense that a religious fiat determining whether or not a woman can control her own reproductive capacities is something which profoundly limits women's liberty and freedom in the name of someone else's religion. So I think we can't think about these issues without thinking of their impacts on individuals – whether they share those religious beliefs or not – and those who would impose their religious beliefs on issues such as abortion need to ask whether people share those religious beliefs or not, or would suffer profoundly on an individual basis.

One issue that has not been raised which I think is important is: if we don't have religion to guide our thinking and our moral decision making what do we have? And, do we need anything? Or, do we just operate as autonomous human beings and call upon what's inside of us to figure that out? And I don't think that is the answer either but we do have guideposts, which neither of the prior speakers has mentioned. We have a, profoundly detailed now actually, system of standards throughout the world that started being formulated after World War II, after the horrors of the Holocaust where the world was brought to attention to see what can happen when governments, in particular the Nazi government of Germany, can run amuck in terms of other human beings' rights or lack thereof. And as a result of the Holocaust the world got together and decided that they had to have some norms to govern human behaviour that weren't religious.

Certainly they are influenced by morality – there is no question about that. Morality comes from religion but we have the Universal Declaration of Human Rights, which is now adhered to by all countries of the world with the exception of fewer than five countries. And out of the Universal Declaration of Human Rights come many other conventions on human rights – conventions that deal with torture, conventions that deal with racism, conventions that deal with equality for women, conventions that deal with landmines, and so on and so forth. And it is these secular signposts, I think, that are advantageous and a far more acceptable way to decide whether behaviour is good or bad or what values should govern curriculum in schools or what values should govern the way in which we conduct wars and so on.  They're all there and I think they are certainly legitimate because the world has agreed to them in large measure.  Now that is not altogether true in the sense that not all conventions are signed on by every country of the world and many of them have reservations but by and large they carry huge legitimacy and moral authority and are the basis for sanctions being applied to countries which are blatant in their violations of human rights be they of women or ethnic groups or racial minorities.  And it seems to me that's where we can find some comfort and some confidence in a moral order that is acceptable in a way, which does not invoke particular religious beliefs even though it may reflect them in some manner.

A word on the perennial subject of pornography and hate speech, I can't sit down without commenting upon that.  Alan has mentioned, rightly so, that pornography when it comes to censorship historically has always been governed by moral standards based in religious concepts.  And this of course has not done women, who are by and large the subject matters of pornography, any service whatsoever because in that equation of good and evil, of course, it was the women who were the evil participant.

People have argued that women's bodies should be covered up and hidden,  that they are dirty, that they incite men to do things that they otherwise wouldn't do and justify all manner of restrictions on their women's liberties.  But is the answer to have no limitations whatsoever on pornography, particularly pornography which sexualizes violence against women and children or pornography which sets out to degrade women and make them subject to ridicule and second class status which degrades their humanity?  I would look to these other standards and say: no, there are other competing interests here.  There are competing rights at play of women's equality so that they have the equal right to speech and to participate in public life, and to be dignified and have equal opportunity in the workplace and not be seen as subjects of male disdain and sexual abuse. So I think that has to weigh in, and similarly on the hate propaganda idea.

Now whether or not the Saskatchewan Human Rights Commission will succeed in an action against an advertiser who is vilifying gay people, I didn't hear Alan say that has gone to tribunal or that there has been evidence called in any deliberation on that point. But the fact that the Saskatchewan Human Rights Commission, whose mandate it is to promote equality should take a stand against such advertisements I don't think is a bad thing. Whether they will win ultimately in the tribunal is another question. I don't think we should in any way resent or deal away Human Rights Commissions whose position it is to protect those who have been historically vilified and marginalized in society simply because of immutable characteristics such as their race or their sexual orientation or their gender. Also bringing that example to an extreme but one which has happened very, very recently in society in Rwanda and Bosnia, hate propaganda was used to great advantage. The massacres that have now been determined, without a shred of a doubt – the massacres in Rwanda could not have taken place without the use of hate propaganda which was used through radio transmissions which were used for several weeks prior to the massacres and the holocaust taking place in Rwanda, because you see they did not have any organized military and they didn't have the weapons needed. What they needed to achieve their goals in Rwanda was for citizens to take up shovels, axes, clubs, whatever they had and go and kill their neighbours. In order to get citizens to do something like that they have to be strongly motivated and now the owners of those radio stations are being prosecuted by the Rwanda war crimes tribunal for their acts of genocide in motivating and inciting that massacre.

Similarly in Bosnia, Human Rights Watch and Amnesty International both have determined that the radio and television broadcasts prior to the early war starting in Bosnia were used extensively to do the same thing – to create an atmosphere and an incentive for the Serbians in Bosnia to take up arms and go and knock down their neighbours' doors. Neighbours who had been their workmates, been their students, been their patients, whatever, and I have talked personally to refugees who have told me that when I was involved in the Bosnian litigation.

So I think it is too easy to say freedom of expression should prevail. Whose expression and to what end?

Thank you.

## · 2 ·

# Maureen Maloney

# ETHICS, LEADERSHIP AND GOVERNMENT[1]

---

It is a great pleasure to be here at this special symposium, and a privilege to have been asked to address this important topic. I hope I will be forgiven, but I have taken the liberty of changing the title of my paper from an affirmative statement [Ethics, Leadership and Government] to an interrogatory one: "How do we get from here to there?"

This is an ambitious topic for 30 or so minutes. I intend to do a brief review of the challenges faced by people in public office, both politicians and senior bureaucrats in attempting to behave ethically. Then I want to share with you my thoughts as to what is being done and what remains to be done: what the priorities should be and what strategies should be adopted to achieve ethical conduct in public life and how leadership will play a large role in doing so. And I hope to do all this without lulling you to sleep!

It is also a propitious time to do such a review.

1. Copyright, M.A. Maloney, 2000. Not for Publication or Quotation Without the Express Permission of the Author. This is a revised and edited version of the speech that was delivered at the Inaugural Symposium of the Sheldon Chumir Foundation on 'Ethics, Leadership and Government' in Calgary in December 2000. Please note that this paper is still very much a work in progress.

Public confidence in public officials is at dangerously low levels,[2] which could have debilitating effects on our democracy. In addition, we have recently launched ourselves into a new century very different from the last. At a time of startling change, dislocation and increasing privatization of public goods and services, ethical standards have become more perplexing and complicated than ever. However, this may also be a time of opportunity for renewal, and for revising the notion of what constitutes the ethical public figure for the 21st century. Let us review briefly the specific ways in which the world has changed over the last century which have contributed to complicating and compounding the challenges that public officials face in the current ethical arena.

### The Old versus New Challenges

The old context in which government operated in the last century was to a large extent and degree much less complicated than the society that current governments now inhabit.

The early part of the last century required a government that created a welcoming society for mainly European immigrants. And in part because of this (but also for a variety of other reasons), it was a society of relatively cohesive values – small communities, nuclear families, with for the most part a Judeo-Christian view of the world and of Canadian society.

The context has changed dramatically. In the words of my favourite poet, Yeats: "a terrible beauty is born." (And I would add, parenthetically, for the most part for the better).

How have these changes manifested themselves?

---

2. This is true more for politicians than for senior public servants. For example in response to a March 1999 poll asking subjects how much they trusted people in various occupations, 45% of citizens said they had "a great deal of trust" in federal public servants, but only 19% answered this way with respect to federal politicians (although it should be mentioned that this was up from 13% in March of 1997). See Ekos Research Associates Inc. "Public Perception on Government and Service" presentation to Workshops on Pride and Recognition in the Public Sector (May 7, 1999 Background Document).

- We have an increasingly multicultural country with new immigrants who bring new values, new languages and new traditions.

- Our population has grown rapidly and we have witnessed a large population shift from rural to urban.

- Technology is simultaneously, and ironically, both shrinking the world, especially for the younger generation, and making it stranger for some, especially the senior generation.

- We have a public demanding more involvement, more knowledge, and more open processes of government.

- We have an increasingly interesting but fractured society of many interest groups, including groups defined by age, sex, culture, economic interest, skin colour, sexual orientation, life experience, religion etc. Government is often perceived to be responding to the loudest interest group.

- There is a faster pace of life.

- A hungry and increasingly monopolistic media is speeding up public discourse, regarding time taken by public officials for reflection as weakness or duplicity. The "if it bleeds, it leads" and racehorse mentality of the media is reducing public discourse of important public issues and relegating complicated public policy debates to 20-second sound bites. Stay tuned; I will have more to say on this important issue later.

Why do these and other changes matter? They are

of the utmost importance. In particular, I believe that these dramatic changes have, in part, contributed to three disturbing themes apparent in the changing relationship between the governing and the governed, which bear directly upon our expectations of politicians and public officials. I do not have the time in this short presentation to do more than raise these issues, but they are clearly worthy of further study and inquiry, as I believe they affect dramatically the ethical standards we set for politicians. All three themes concern the changing relationship between the governing and the governed.

The first issue which troubles me is the increasing tendency of governments, aided by a willing public, to deal with the public as "consumers" or "customers"[3] rather than as "citizens," which changes the discourse between the governing and governed to one of complaint or satisfaction rather than that of a social contract under which both owe important responsibilities and accountabilities. "Ask not what your country can do for you, but what you can do for your country," the former United States of America President John F. Kennedy's famous admonition now seems like a sentimental moment from a bygone era.

The responsibility of citizens is little discussed and even less practiced. Everyone is a potential client or victim of government activity. Citizens have come to be viewed as the objects of government policy, instead of (please excuse the pun) *subjects* in whose collective interests government's activities are carried out. This approach can have significant consequences. For example, government actions, which expose a few citizens to some small risk to bring significant benefits to many, are now portrayed as at best reprehensible, and at worst unforgivable. In some circumstances both reactions may be warranted, but surely not all. Good governance is often the art of weighing competing claims and benefits and making decisions in the best interests of the entire community. (On a parenthetical note, the very nature of who

3. For a good discussion of this topic and why this should not be allowed to happen see Henry Mintzberg in the May-June, 1996 <u>Harvard Business Review</u> at p.75.

or what is considered "community" is also getting murkier and murkier, and often seems to be getting lost in the cacophony of post-modernism – an essay for another day). The second disturbing theme, in part a natural outgrowth of the first, is the emerging debate as to whether public services would be delivered more effectively and efficiently if politicians and their senior officials were permitted to act more like their counterparts in the private sector. In its purest form, such a policy would presumably result in government activities being governed by the "invisible hand" of self-interest embraced by private enterprise. In effect, this would mean a complete reversal of the traditional (and up until now, sacrosanct) duty owed by public officials to act in the public interest.

Taken to its limits, this could lead to allowing public officials to deliver public goods and services in such a manner as to further their own self-interest, the theory being that such practice would result in the optimum use and delivery of public goods, in the same way that private enterprise does with private goods. Put in these terms, the idea, of course, sounds preposterous. However, in a much more subtle form, this is happening increasingly in Canada as an ever-growing number of government services become privatized. Clearly private companies are operating in their own and not the public interest; indeed, they are legislated to do so by corporate law. However, if public goods and services are being delivered (e.g. prison operations, social services), the public must demand certain ethical operating standards.

What ethical standards should be required in such cases? This is an issue requiring considerable thought and attention. Moreover, as an increasing number of public services are privatized, the question may be posed that if private companies are allowed to act in their own self-interest while providing public services (albeit with some contractual caveats), then why shouldn't governments and their officials be allowed to act in their own self-interest in directing and operating public services, as they are more clearly accountable through the electoral process? I raise this issue as one of concern for future reflection. For the purposes of this speech, and in keeping with my own philosophy for the reasons enunciated later, I assume that the duty of governmental officials to act in the public interest is, and should remain, of paramount importance to public office.

The third major change in the relationship between the citizenry and the government is that in the complex world we inhabit, there is often no consensus on major policy issues that involve, to some extent, moral and ethical underpinnings. For issues such as war, gay rights, abortion, or treaty rights and entitlement, there is simply NO clear moral consensus on how governments should respond ethically and morally. There is no moral compass. Discussions of ethical and moral decision-making all too often descend into positional bargaining devoid of moral content, which further undermines the legitimacy of the governments and politicians making those decisions.

Having all too briefly outlined what I perceive to be three important elements of the changing relationship between citizens and their governments which directly impact on our ideal of ethical conduct, I shall now turn to whether – and to what extent – society has a shared notion of what constitutes ethical conduct.

Some of the usual values associated with ethical conduct are neatly summarized by Tait:[4] integrity, honesty, probity, prudence, impartiality, equity, disinterestedness, and discretion. One has to ask, of course, what singles out politicians and public officials from other professionals with respect to standards of ethical behaviour? The answer is easy to articulate, but harder to implement.

As Tait states, "What makes [politicians and public officials] distinctive from other professions is the intersec-

4. John Tait, Report of the Deputy Minister's Task Force on Public Service Values and Ethics, available at http://www.ccmd-ccg.gc.ca/publications_e.html, p16.

tion with the democratic and professional values of public service. Integrity, for example, is required in all professions. Its distinctiveness in the public service lies in the capacity to hold a public trust and to put the common good ahead of any private interest or advantage."[5]

Let us start then with that basic understanding. The essence of ethical conduct by public officials is to subordinate their own self-interest for the public good. And this is a *sine qua non* upon which democracies are founded. Each public official, on taking office (elected or appointed), must understand the public trust that they are undertaking.[6] And to exhibit ethical conduct is crucial, because as Fleischman points out, it provides for the public

> ...the sure knowledge that public policy is being made for the benefit of the public, the greatest good of the greatest number over the long run. All will, indeed, sacrifice their respective interests if they are told and can wholeheartedly believe, that such sacrifice is necessary and its particular incidence – the degree to which it falls disparately upon different social interests in the short run – is required by the long run good of all.[7]

Whether this ideal remains fully true in our increasingly atomistic, individualistic, self-interested, consumer-driven and fractured society is one of the questions I would like to pose. I have no definitive answer. This caveat notwithstanding, self-interested behaviour on the part of public officials clearly poses dangers to democracy, and of the most corrosive kind. Again, to quote Fleischman:

Nothing – not errors of judgment, not waste,

5. Tait, ibid.

6. Or as proposed by Max Weber, they must have "an ethics of responsibility" which encompasses three qualities: passion, a feeling of responsibility, and a sense of proportion. See Max Weber, " Politics as a Vocation," in From Max Weber, trans. H. Gerth and C.W. Mills (New York: Oxford University Press, 1958), pp.77-158.

7. Joel L. Fleishman, "The Pursuit of Self-Interest for the Public Good: An Ethical Paradox of Representative Democracy", Ethics and Government, Earl Warren Conference 1982, (The Roscoe Pound-American Trial Lawyers Association Foundation), p27.

not inefficiency, not high taxes, not over regulation, not even the loss of a war – so
shakes representative government at its root
as does a belief by the public that officials
who govern act chiefly out of concern for private self-interest rather than the public interest of those who elected them.[8]

This is particularly disturbing in our present context,
as I believe there is an increasing perception by the public
that politicians act in their own self-interest. I should make
it clear that I do not mean to suggest that the majority of the
public perceives that politicians are lining their own pockets
(although I suspect that a not-insignificant minority do
share this view), but that a majority do believe that politicians act in their own self-interest by pursuing the interests
of their particular political party in order to perpetuate their
term in power for power itself rather than any desire to act
on behalf of, and in, the public interest. This notion was put
more colourfully and succinctly to me by a fellow passen-
ger on a train in India some years ago. Commenting on his
reason for not having voted in the previous election, he
remarked: "It doesn't matter whom you vote for, the government always wins."

This is one of the main contributing factors (if not
*the* contributing factor) to the public's lack of faith in governments in Canada today. How has this happened? And
how can we renew the public faith in public officials?

I believe that as the consensus on public policy
issues, particularly those in the moral arena, has collapsed,
there has been an increasing focus on those who are actually making controversial decisions. Accordingly, the conduct of public officials is under scrutiny as never before.
The search to uncover ethical impurity seems at times to
have become a predominant occupation. But the world of
morality is a confusing and perplexing one these days. As

8. Fleischman, ibid. pp.26-27

Langford asks: "Can any public official say with any authority where the line is between good and bad behaviour?"[9]

Professor Langford illustrates his point by exploring the nature of the oath of confidentially which public servants are required to take upon appointment to office. Confidentiality has always been deemed essential to ensure the requisite degree of trust between public servants and Ministers of the Crown. The oath of confidentiality allows Ministers and public servant advisors to speak freely and frankly in the knowledge that hasty or ill-conceived options or ideas will not be relayed to the public prematurely before careful consideration can be given to them. In recent times, this ideal of trust between the politician and public servant advisor is under considerable attack. Indeed, confidentiality, once the hallmark of loyalty to a public sector employer, is now regularly portrayed as an offence against the public's right to know. Whistle blowing is now actively encouraged.[10]

The ethical ground is shifting so rapidly and in many competing directions, that it is not surprising that public officials are increasingly unable to distinguish right from wrong.

To illustrate the difficulty of painting bright lines delineating ethical conduct, I will focus on the area of conflict of interest. Conflict of interest is at the very core of the public official's ethical duty, and one often in the news, certainly in BC and also in the most recent federal election. In recent years, Langford tells us, "conflict of interest has been transformed from a venal sin to a crime seemingly second only in magnitude to mass murder."[11]

Most people believe that conflict of interest issues are relatively straightforward for public officials. Not so. Indeed, some public offices have inherent conflict built into the duties.

9. These comments and ideas are taken from an overview content piece of a presentation by Professor John Langford, "The Mad, Mad World of Public Morality" for the B.C. Government's Executive Development Program, Dunsmuir Lodge, February 18,1996 (unpublished).
10. The irony here, of course, is that even though it is actively encouraged, the public servant is rarely protected from the consequences of such whistle blowing if discovered. For most public servants this means, as my mother would say: "you can't win for losing".
11. Langford, supra. 9.

Take, for example, elected MPs or MLAs. As members of Parliament or of a legislature, they have to represent not only the interests of their constituents, but also those of the entire country or province. Different interests may collide between these two, and indeed among varying constituents. Legislators are expected to represent, compromise, and respond to a variety of conflicting interests. But how do we know when this discretion has been exercised appropriately?

Some examples may elucidate the difficulties. There are three types of conflict of interest.[12]

1. *Inherent Self-Interest.* This arises where, for example, members of parliament vote on their own salaries and pensions as holders of the public purse. Personally, I believe this should be sent to an independent body in much the same way as judicial salaries are now set. Yet this runs counter to one of the most important duties parliaments and legislatures carry out, and for which they are accountable: the expenditure of public funds.

2. *Politically Mandated Conflict.* Consider, for example, a legislator who is also a farmer. She has been voted in by her farming constituents to represent their interests. What happens when she votes for increased farming subsidies? She could abstain from voting, of course, but what of the interests of her constituents? Does it mean that they do not get a voice or vote on an issue of vital importance to them? Are ethics relative to numbers? Would it make a difference if only ten specialized farmers would benefit from

---

12. I found this useful taxonomy in The Honorable Richardson Preyer, "Legislative Ethics", Ethics and Government, supra 7, p.53 ff.

the subsidy and the legislator is one of them? What if she would not benefit personally but her three close friends would?

3. *Personally Necessary Conflicts.* These are the most usual conflicts that are highlighted in the media. They relate to income or assets that an MP owns, the divestiture of which is impossible (the house one lives in) or which would cause hardship (the family company one owns). We now have a plethora of laws (with relative degrees of complexity, sophistication and coverage), which attempt both to define and give guidance on these thorny issues. In many ways, of the three types of conflict, this is the one more readily amenable to codification. But even direct self-interest is becoming difficult to ascertain.

As we have seen, it is not easy to identify conflicts that arise out of past and present affairs or conduct. It is much more difficult to work out when the conflict could relate to a future interest or income.

There is much more movement between the private and public sectors today than there has ever been in the past. Some of this is prompted by more easily interchangeable skills, greater mobility, and fluidity of careers, which to some extent has been accelerated by government downsizing. However these useful interchanges have also given rise to concerns over the influences that could potentially affect government decision-makers.

Again, some examples may illuminate the point. Consider the following cases:

1. A government technology expert heads a

panel recommending which tender bid should be accepted for a multi-million dollar contract. The firm which is offered the contract makes an offer to this same government employee six months later at triple her salary, which she accepts.

Has the government employee acted appropriately? Would it make a difference if it were one day, one week or one year later that the job is offered? Is ethical conduct relative to the time expired? Does conflict have to do more these days with perception rather than reality?

2. A lawyer who is the Chair of an administrative tribunal resigns his position to engage in private practice, which includes appearing for clients before the very tribunal on which he served.

3. The CEO of a regulatory agency that makes lucrative and sensitive licensing decisions resigns her government position to work for a major company, the recipient of many positive license decisions from her.

4. A former cabinet minister is appointed to several boards of companies who were given large subsidies by his ministry when he was a cabinet minister.

All of these are the types of instances that arise in the governments of this country. Clearly they give rise to the potential for the appearance of conflict, if not actual conflict. Should there then be a code prohibiting such conduct? What then of the value of the interchange between the private and public sectors? What then of the ability of certain skilled people to accept offers from people who have witnessed their skills at close hand, which has been the sole reason for the job offer? These illustrations raise very clearly the need for guidelines in advance. There are no immutable standards. Accordingly, standards must be set which meet the conflicting public interests of (1) ensuring public officials are willing to stand for, or be appointed to, office, and (2) eliminating the possibility of a public official's acting in his or her own self-interest rather than the public interest when delegated to make important decisions.

What then should be the standards?

At one end of the spectrum is conduct that is criminal and therefore clearly unethical. Yet this can hardly be our yardstick. As Fleischman has said:

> The single most important fact about the ethics of public officials is the extremely narrow range of conduct to which the legal sanction can conceivably extend. Laws penalizing bribery, misuse of public office, and pecuniary conflict of interest are obviously essential safeguards against the venality of crooked officials, but it does not follow that, without more, simple abstention from criminal conduct makes a public official ethical.[13]

If we rely only on criminal conduct, we have not much worth preserving.

At the other end of the spectrum, we encounter conduct that is clearly ethical. We have the story of U.S. President Jefferson who, upon receiving a gift from a Baltimore merchant, promptly returned it with the attached note:

13. Fleishman, supra 7, p.27.

It is the law, sacred to me while in public character, to receive nothing which bears a pecuniary value. This is necessary to the confidence of my country, it is necessary as an example for its benefit, and necessary to the tranquillity of my own mind.[14]

Or, closer to home, there is the legendary tale of Alex McDonald, the former B.C. Attorney General who, upon being elected to office, received a large basket of food and drinks from a local brewer with whom he was acquainted. He returned the basket with the note: "If the basket is a gift, it is too generous, if a bribe it is not enough."

It is, of course, the grey area in the middle that poses the most difficulty for public officials and governments alike, particularly as the area appears to expand and contract depending upon the circumstances.

How can guidance be provided? As Peter Drucker said, "the best way to predict the future is to create it." Here are my five suggestions as to how to do just that.

## 1. Codes of conduct, proper selection, and training and education

Clearly, laws or codes of conduct that not only set out clear principles, but also attempt to particularize and predict as many specific circumstances as possible, are imperative. There must also be an independent ethics advisor to assist those who require guidance, and to make findings of unethical conduct when appropriate.

However, we should not place all our ethical eggs in the codification basket. Public office demands much more. Several strategies must be put in place. In particular, careful recruitment (and election?) of officials is imperative. Education and training of all public officials is also vital. As

14. Ibid. p.28.

H.G. Wells said, in a very different context: "Human history becomes more and more a race between education and catastrophe"[15]

## 2. Citizen involvement, and more interactive government

In order to encourage citizenship values of responsibility and obligation, government must involve citizens more clearly in public policy formation. Government must become much more transparent and open. Processes must be developed to ensure that citizens have the opportunity to participate in important government decisions, especially those decisions that directly affect their lives and interests.

Accordingly, government must change the way in which it makes important decisions, by increasing transparency and accountability of decision-making. Some of these issues have been – and continue to be – addressed by freedom of information and privacy laws. And governments are to be commended for taking these steps. However, more could and should be done. As former Chief Justice Brandeis of the US Supreme Court once remarked: "Sunlight is the best of disinfectants; electric light the most efficient policeman."

Shining a bright light on the workings of government is of a two-fold and two-way benefit. The public is assured that the government is working in the public interest; and if not, the public will find out. In addition, it secures to the government an important degree of accountability and therefore legitimacy. Furthermore, engaging citizens in debates around important public policy decisions will allow them to more fully appreciate the complexities of particular decisions, and how and why certain conclusions or solutions were reached. Such engagement should reduce the suspicion that frequently surrounds controversial decisions,

15. Herbert George Wells, The Outline of History (1951 ed., ch. 40).

as to whether the decision was reached arbitrarily, in igno-rance of all the facts, or because of unknown special inter-ests.  In addition it will help foster the responsibilities of cit-izens to their society.  On the other hand it will ensure that government is fully apprised of all the facts and perspec-tives before making a difficult decision, and place an obli-gation on it to give cogent and rational reasons for the deci-sions they reach.

On a different note, I believe that the impersonal-ized face of government has also contributed to the mis-trust of public officials.  In our complex and growing socie-ty, increasing numbers of people work for government, and one result of this has been the creation of organizational structures where people rarely interact with senior public officials who are responsible for making public policy and operational recommendations. Another concern, partly, but not entirely, grown out of the increasing size of govern-ment, is the often impersonal manner in which government officials interface with citizens, in particular the growing use of bureaucratic language and the red tape associated with applying for or complying with government programs.

The irony here, of course, is that the laws and reg-ulations that attempt to secure sound public management, ethical behaviour and accountability are some of the rea-sons people feel they are being drowned in red tape or not being treated appropriately.  The lack of face-to-face accountability has had a negative effect upon the promo-tion of ethics and a reciprocal understanding of the issues facing both government officials and citizens.  Much more effort and consideration should be paid to reorganizing the way public decisions and services are conceived and deliv-ered in order to reverse this lamentable trend.  A good example of this was the creation of the Commission on Resources and Environment in British Columbia, which proved to be an excellent model for participatory decision-making.

## 3. The role of the media

The fourth estate, the media, has a vital, indeed crucial, role to play in ensuring that government officials are held to account. However, it is a role that requires responsibility and obligation. The media must spend time and resources to ensure thorough and accurate investigation and reporting – a crucial pillar of any democracy. They must resist the temptation for sensational, entertainment-style, or "gotcha" journalism. Occasionally, in the haste to report the story first, the press jumps to impetuous conclusions and a public official is castigated and condemned weeks before any hearing or ruling is made on his or her conduct. As surgeons have warned throughout the ages, "amputation without diagnosis: the result is always a casualty." The press must play the role of honest broker between government and the public, rooting out unethical conduct but ensuring that both sides are told. Accordingly, it is imperative that the media should explore their own ethical responsibilities as to how allegations are reported and researched. This is an integral part of the democratic system.

## 4. Leadership

And, finally, what of the individual responsibility to conduct oneself ethically? Ethical behaviour has not only to do with laws and codes setting out the required conduct. As I have already mentioned there is an increasing emphasis on translating ethical behaviour into laws: conflict laws, disclosure laws, freedom of information and privacy laws, and financial management and accountability acts. And whilst this is a necessary condition, it is not a sufficient condition. We cannot legalize morality or character. To do so runs the risk of equating ethical conduct with obeying the law.

Ethical character is much broader than a consideration of the myriad controls placed on the behaviour of public officials. Strong demonstrations of ethical leadership by politicians play a crucial role in securing ethical behaviour by others. Actions speak louder than words. As George Bernard Shaw said, "the greatest reformers the world has ever seen are those who commence upon themselves."

And how does one acquire these leadership abilities? It has to do with that old-fashioned concept of "character". Ethics without character, in the words of Shakespeare, are "a loud sounding nothing". And how do we produce character? There is a touching short story named *The Mask*. As Fleischman tells it,

> It is about a young man desperately in love with a woman. He is not very handsome, so he has a very handsome, lifelike mask made and wears it over many years of courtship. He has won her love, at last, when one of his competitors for her love in a desperate and despicable move tells her that the successful suitor is, in fact, wearing a mask. In a dramatic climax, he is unmasked, and to the surprise of all, most of all himself, his face underneath the mask is identical with the mask, having been molded by the years of wear.[16]

Perhaps Woodrow Wilson encapsulated the moral of the story succinctly with his famous reply when asked how do we produce character: "Character is a by-product; it is produced in the great manufacture of daily duty."[17]

I will conclude this speech with one of my favourite quotes, which may sum up some of the at times contradic-

16. This story is related by Fleischman, supra 7, at p.32.
17. Ibid. at p33.

tory themes in my speech regarding the current state of ethics, leadership and government.  According to novelist and essayist James B. Cabell, "the optimist proclaims that we live in the best of all possible worlds, and the pessimist fears this is true."[18]

Thank you for listening.

18. James Branch Cabell, The Silver Stallion (1926)

· 3 ·
## Peter Desbarats

# MEDIA ETHICS IN THE AGE OF MULTIMEDIA:
## The Real Meaning of Convergence

---

That we live in a time of rapid technological change is definitely not news, nor is the fact that the news business, the business of journalism, is one those enterprises most affected by this change, existing as it does at one of the main intersections of computer and communications technologies. But every now and then, in our personal histories, something happens that seems to capture and crystallize the process of change for each of us. For me, one of those insightful times occurred last summer as I finished the last of four interviews with the publishers of Toronto's major daily newspapers for a research project undertaken by friends of mine at Laval University in Quebec.

To each publisher I put the assertion that from now on the success of a newspaper will be measured by its success in meeting the challenge of adaptation to the Internet. To my surprise, all four publishers agreed with this statement without a moment's hesitation. And that experience has come to symbolize for me the death of the newspaper industry, as I had known it for half a century. For this wasn't just the usual theorizing about new information media. This was laid down as an operating principle for anyone in the media business today – that the commercial value of a newspaper now depends on its perceived potential as a site or portal on the Internet. In fact, a few months later, we saw this principle being applied in the huge purchase of Conrad Black's Hollinger newspapers by Asper and Son of CanWest Global. Since the deal became final a few weeks ago, Leonard Asper, Izzy Asper's son and President and CEO of CanWest Global, has talked constantly about the importance of the newspapers as potential content providers for Canwest's television and Internet operations, and not at all about the value and importance of the newspapers themselves.

So that's one of my themes today – convergence, what it means for the business of journalism and what, in fact, is the business of journalism? But before I deal with that, I want to talk briefly about another and more personal kind of convergence – the coming together after a lifetime as a journalist, journalism educator and journalism critic of many of the impressions and opinions that I've formed over the years. I find, as you get older that a process of simplification occurs – that you realize that certain basic truths not only have stood up to experience but have been confirmed by it.

As far as I can recall, I started my intellectual life as a teen-ager with the half-baked idea that art or artistic expression is the most important human activity. And now, half a century later, I know that it is. And related to that is the belief that journalism at its best, real journalism, is one of those arts. And out of that very personal and simple belief, if you transform it into practice, emerges a revolutionary approach to journalism in which media owners are seen to exist primarily to support the art of journalism and its practitioners, not the other way around. And this concept of journalism as art also provides a way to evaluate and influence the upheaval that technology is creating in the world of media. It's important to clearly identify journalism as an art because one of the essential characteristics of art is truth. There simply cannot be a dishonest or false work of art and the same thing applies to a work of journalism.

I warned you that these notions of the primacy of art in human activity, and the artistic character of journalism, are revolutionary because most people in my experience would scoff at the notion of truth as a defining characteristic of journalism. I don't know how many times, since I assumed a Chair of Media Ethics at Ryerson Polytechnic University, I've had to listen to the predictable jokes about ethical journalism being an oxymoron. But in reality, false or cheap or unethical journalism is the contradiction in terms. Not only is good journalism essential to the proper functioning of our society, but only good journalism in the long run will ensure the survival and prosperity of significant media enterprises.

Never mind all the glib popular rankings of journalists along with lawyers and politicians at the bottom of the sincerity and credibility graphs in public opinion polls. How meaningful are they when compared with the thousands of journalists a year who are threatened, fired, imprisoned, tortured, killed in action or assassinated in the course of their work? And this is the proud, bloody heritage of the journalism that I am discussing today, not the media empires and fortunes that have been created from the work and sometimes the lives of journalists. In all the lists that are published every year of journalists who have suffered and died in the fight for freedom of expression, I have rarely seen the names of media owners whose rare sacrifices for journalism consist of occasional losses in the stock market.

At the other end of the journalistic spectrum we have not tabloid journalism – the usual opposition between serious and popular journalism – but what I will call for lack of a better term industrial journalism. This is journalism treated strictly as a commercial product or commodity as opposed to journalism regarded as a work of art inextricably linked with humankind's search for freedom of expression and political freedom. Keeping this distinction in mind will help us to keep our ethical bearings as we move deeper, in this lecture and in reality, into the accelerating technological tornado that is already altering the media landscape almost beyond recognition and, as many people have said, changing the very definition of journalism.

Considering the pace of innovation in computers and communications in recent decades, it's hard for many of us to appreciate that we are still in the early stages of the information revolution. It was only 20 years ago that I served on the Royal Commission on Newspapers and wrote a research report on Newspapers and Computers, but it seems as if a century has passed since then. It's hard to believe that none of the high-priced experts that I consulted in Toronto, New York, London and Paris in 1980 had any notion of the Internet or anything like it. We all believed in those days that the home computer screen would be the main source of print, audio and video information, not the primitive computers that were then used in most Canadian newspapers and that were finding their way into offices and a few homes. So experience warns us against assuming that the computers and communications systems that our children will be using in the year 2020 will be anything like today's systems.

Experience also tells us, however, that the Internet in some form is here to stay, that its use will continue to increase and that any field such as journalism that relies on gathering and distributing information will be strongly affected. The current issue of the *New Yorker*, devoted to

The Digital Age, contains an article on advances in fiber optic networking technology that quotes "knowledgeable people" as predicting that these advances "will quickly increase the Internet's output of data by a factor of a thousand or more." It forecasts that the Internet will become the "Evernet" – "available to us anywhere, anytime," that it will create enormous new wealth, and that it will alter the way we "live, work, seek pleasure, and gather together."

We've all been reading this kind of thing for years but with diminishing skepticism. We are now aware of the power of these technologies; most of us have been intimately affected by them. It's as if we are rushing at an accelerating rate into some sort of technological "black hole" of such immense energy that no one can predict what sort of global society will emerge from this process.

The mysterious black holes of astronomy are, fortunately, something we observe only from a distance. But we are already entering the black hole of communications and computer technologies. What occurs inside that process can be and must be influenced by us, starting with an assessment of the structures and methods in place as we enter the tornado.

In the field of news media this is relatively easy because, at least so far, mergers and consolidation of media organizations have accompanied advances in computers and communications on an unprecedented scale. In 1981, when the Royal Commission on Newspapers issued its report, Canada's newspaper industry was already the most concentrated in the western world. From 1970 to 1980, the share of daily newspaper circulation that was independently owned had decreased from 40 to 25 percent in English Canada, and from 50 to 10 percent in Quebec. In each of these two communities, three major chains controlled the remainder.

The Royal Commission predicted that more concentration would occur unless prevented by law. That's exactly what happened. Today the few remaining independently owned daily newspapers account for an insignificant share of circulation. The rest is divided nationally between three chains – CanWest Global, Quebecor which also owns the Sun group in English-speaking Canada and the Power Corporation in Quebec which has just purchased three urban dailies from Conrad Black to add to its ownership of *La Presse* in Montreal. Thomson's last major newspaper, *The Globe and Mail,* is now part of the BCE multi-media empire leaving the *Toronto Star* as the last independently owned daily in Toronto, although the Star itself has created, in self-defense, a mini-chain in Ontario incorporating Hamilton and Kitchener dailies.

But there is one significant difference between the situation in 1980 and today. Despite a degree of concentration in newspapers that would have seemed extreme even by the relaxed standards of 1980, the recent consolidations have occurred with almost no significant reaction from the public, from government or even from journalists.

There seem to be at least three reasons for this. The first is that concentration of media ownership has also continued in the United States and in many other developed countries so that it's now considered to be "normal" and inevitable. The second, and perhaps more important, is that the technical "convergence" of print, radio and television in a single data stream on the Internet is being regarded as a parallel and linked process to the convergence of ownership in the hands of a few giant corporations. To put it the other way around: concentration of media ownership is now regarded as just as inevitable as media convergence on the Internet. And in the background is a third contributor to public apathy – the unproven belief or hope that the Internet by its nature will promote a more diverse and democratic media world at some point in the future.

But the most recent and alarming development in Canadian journalism has been the sudden appearance and acceptance of cross-ownership as a result of CanWest's purchase of the Hollinger newspapers. Something that was not tolerated previously, except in a few isolated cases, apparently has become legitimate without any public discussion of any kind.

Of course the CRTC has more than cross-ownership to worry about these days as digital radio and TV in combination with the Internet threaten to destroy the foundations of its regulatory authority. And I understand, as I said at the beginning, that technological convergence is making media concentration seem inevitable. But it's remarkable that someone like Leonard Asper now boasts about concentration and convergence without even paying lip service to benefits of diversity and competition in journalism. Has that concept suddenly become totally irrelevant?

Is it unimportant when Leonard Asper, in the AOL interview I cited earlier, boasts that "between the TV stations and papers we have an unprecedented share of the total ad pie" as well as "a tremendous opportunity to cross promote each other which will result in increased ratings in TV and increased circulation for the newspaper". Does Mr. Asper really believe that cross-promotion has no editorial or political consequences? Does he actually think that when Peter Kent of Global TV promotes a story that will run in the *National Post* the next day, as he has been doing recently, this doesn't create in the minds of viewers a close identification between Global and the highly political and partisan *National Post*?

When Mr. Asper states that he will break new ground by applying the principles of the Broadcasting Act to the many newspapers that he now controls, requiring their editors to publish a newspaper "that reflects the community it serves and provides balance in its opinion pieces," doesn't he understand that this is a policy that has vast political implications?

And why wasn't this policy communicated to his father whose statement on last week's federal election, urging Canadians to vote for a minority government, was published in many of the CanWest newspapers without any indication of Izzy Asper's long and continuing connection to the Liberal party? I'm citing Leonard Asper here but the ideas that he expresses are common to the leaders of our emerging multi-media empires.

From a manufacturing point of view, this makes sense.  If newsrooms were producing widgets, why not recycle the same widgets in various media?  Isn't that synergy?  But after all his experience with television news, Mr. Asper apparently still doesn't understand the first thing about journalism.  There are at least two things wrong with his scenario.

First, initial experience has shown that this type of synergy doesn't always work. Recently I moderated a panel discussion in which the young editor of a major Canadian newspaper's web page explained why he required a separate staff of about a dozen journalists. "When I sit in on the paper's daily editorial meeting," he said, "they're all talking about their plans for tomorrow's paper.  By the time they've produced their stories, those same stories have been on my web site for hours.  We can't afford to wait for them.  We have to get the stories ourselves, and update them ourselves."

Second, and most important, the best journalism isn't a manufactured product but an act of creative artistry.  Like all artistic endeavors, journalism is a highly individual activity that flourishes under special conditions and that defies the rules of industrial productivity. You cannot create great paintings on an assembly line; management committees do not inspire great journalism. It is created by individual journalists who are inspired by individual editors and publishers.

It's strange that Mr. Asper hasn't realized this because he has, as part of CanWest's empire, a half-share of the most recent and one of the most striking examples of this axiom – the *National Post*. Since it first appeared several years ago, the *National Post* has been an extraordinary, magnificent, anachronistic anomaly on the North American newspaper scene. Like all the great newspapers of yesteryear, it is the creation of an individual publisher with a clear personal and political agenda. And the decision to launch it flew in the face of conventional business wisdom.

That Conrad Black blithely ignored some of the basic principles of good journalism in the process of producing some great journalism was part of the excitement. No one would describe the Post's news coverage of the recent federal election – never mind its opinion pieces – as fair and balanced. It was outrageously partisan, a temporary and wonderful throwback to an earlier era when publishers were often politicians and their newspapers competed vigorously, and not always ethically, against one another.

But as I said, Conrad Black is an anachronism within an anachronism, a Citizen Kane figure in an unusual Toronto newspaper world of four competitive dailies representing not only four different approaches to politics but four different journalistic traditions. This cannot last. Already the *Toronto Sun* has become part of a huge media empire based in Montreal, the old family names appear to be fading from the *Toronto Star*, and both the Globe and the Post are part of shareholder-owned multi-media conglomerates where profit and not journalistic passion is the primary motivating factor. In that kind of bureaucratic atmosphere, journalists tend to become content providers and real journalism dies.

That's what is happening across North America and that's why media observers such as myself have started to wonder if the black hole of technological change might contain the seeds of a more promising future for journalism.

Analogies are treacherous, particularly between worlds as diverse as journalism and astrophysics, but we do know that periods of rapid change in any field of human endeavor, whether it's technology, politics or art, liberate immense amounts of creative energy, just as the ordinary material of the universe being sucked into black holes creates almost unimaginable outputs of energy through processes that physicists still do not understand. It's certainly possible to speculate that future changes in computers and communications technologies will be powerful enough to break up the stultifying media organizations of today, the huge factories where industrial journalism is produced, and to create conditions where many different types of journalists can practice the art of journalism within new types of structures. And if we look hard enough today, and watch what some younger journalists are trying to do on the Internet, we can see a few signs of this actually happening.

## · 4 ·

## Bob Rae

# IN DEFENSE OF POLITICS[1]

I want to talk to you tonight and to try to get us back to some basics, because I know this is the way Sheldon would have liked to talk about it. I want to talk to you tonight a little bit about the basics of politics.

I know that to talk of politics and ethics in the same sentence seems to many of you like an exercise in wishful thinking at best, because there is something in our popular culture which tells us that politics is immoral and dirty and unethical, and that high minded and ethical people should have nothing to do with it.

In fact, I have often told the story of a friend of mine who, many years ago, was telling me about a discussion she was having within her family. She was saying, "You know, I had a really tough choice. I could have handled this in a straightforward, honest way, or I could have been really political about it." I looked at her and said, "Thank you very, very much for your endorsement!"

---

1. This chapter is prepared, with only minor editing, from the symposium tapes.

But my message to you tonight is very simple.  It is that politics is indeed a messy business.  It is not clean, in the sense that it is not *neat*.

But on the other hand, life itself is not neat.  It does not lend itself to simple categories, as we all learn as we get older and, I hope, wiser.  And politics is necessary, and in fact it is inevitable.  It is impossible to imagine any kind of social relationship without politics being a necessary and clear feature of it.

Robinson Crusoe did not have to worry about politics until Friday came along, and at that point politics became very important to Robinson Crusoe.  (I would suspect it became even more important to Friday).  I hesitate, in the context of the election, to talk about Adam and Eve who, if I believe what I have read in the papers, live somewhere near Drumheller.  But it is fair for us to assume that Adam was blissfully unaware of politics until Eve came along (and I mean this semi-seriously).  Because as soon as you have a relationship between two people, you have a political relationship.  And as someone who lives in a family of five, I can assure you it is a *very* political relationship!  (Our family is, I suppose, some kind of feminist democracy of which I am a minority of one).

Politics is about power.  We all know that is what defines the political game whether it is between men and women, whether it is within families, whether it is within offices, or whether it is within, dare I say, law firms.  However it is expressed, it is about who gets what, when, where and how – to use the classic phrase.

But politics is also inevitable because of the kinds of beings that people are.  Politics is about values.  It has to be about values, because as soon as people learn to talk, we have to talk about the legitimacy of the power relationship that exists between us.  And we come to terms with the fact that every relationship has a language to describe it and, in fact, even ascribing something as simple as authority or legitimacy to those who are in power, we are in a sense defining that relationship in terms of values, in terms of ethics.

You are more or less listening to me. I don't know what you are doing or where your minds are but you certainly are looking at me. But I do know I have no control over that. You are ascribing to me (however temporarily) a certain respect, deference, authority, whatever you want to call it, because of the values we have all grown up with. We all recognize that if you invite someone as a guest to come and talk to you, then you listen to what he has to say (more or less), and in that sense I have a political relationship with you. It doesn't last very long. And if I were to attempt to abuse it, by actually telling you to do something, or asserting my authority to try to bring out some form of behaviour, I would be taking a major risk, because you might not do it, in which case my legitimacy would suddenly collapse.

The reason I give you this simple example is to remind you that politics is about power. It is about legitimacy. It is inevitably about values, and everyone likes to think that they don't engage in politics. In fact, I now have to call myself a "recovering" politician.

Well, now I am almost completely recovered. But about the legitimacy of the enterprise there can be no doubt. Al Gore and George Bush are now engaged in a systemic argument about the legitimacy of their respective endeavours to become the President of the United States, in what has to be one of the most extraordinary television programs I think we have all watched this month.

I only met Sheldon Chumir once. I wish I had known him better, and wish I had got to know him longer. But I think all of you in this room know that he understood better than anyone that politics is about ideas and about values as much as it is about what we think of as root power. And, in fact, values and ideas can have more impact – if well articulated – than anybody might think.

It was Sheldon's preoccupation with values and ideas that brought him into politics. I don't think he ever saw himself as somebody who had to become Premier or had to be the exerciser of formal authority. He didn't see that as being necessary in order for him to have an impact and to make a difference. He understood the power of an idea, and the power of debates about ideas. It was his commitment to principles, and to a debate marked by passion, respect and, if I may say so humour, that led him from a successful law practice and a very successful business career to a political life that was tragically cut short by his bout with cancer.

I think (and maybe I am presuming too much in even suggesting such a thing) Sheldon would have taken a rather dim view of the political experience that we have just been through. When I was asked to suggest what I would talk about, it was before either Marsha or Joel[2] or I knew there was going to be an election or that we would have just recovered from an election. And so when a number of you came up to me tonight and said you were looking forward to my remarks "in defense of politics," there was a sense of bemusement about the comment. Because we have just been through a rather extraordinary exercise, which I think gives us an opportunity to reflect on the nature and the culture of politics at the moment in Canada and what we can do about it to make it better.

I am not a cynic. I don't believe we should sit back and simply make fun of what has taken place. I think we should have some fun with it, because it does represent an element, I suppose, of humour – but we do have to contend with the challenges that it leaves with us.

We have just emerged from an election campaign which was supposed to be, according to the opening statements on all sides, about respect and values. And I must

---

2. References here are to Marsha Hanen, President of the Sheldon Chumir Foundation for Ethics in Leadership, and Joel Bell, chair of the Board of the Sheldon Chumir Foundation.

say it very quickly moved into a brawl of name-calling and negativity. Fewer Canadians voted than ever before, and that is hardly surprising.

As some of you may have heard from my comments on the radio last week, I was asked to talk about politics without talking very much about the election, which was quite a feat I can assure you. One of the things I suggested was to try to understand what has happened to the political process. Just imagine for a moment if General Motors, Ford, Chrysler, Honda and Toyota proceeded to engage in a systematic campaign of denigration of the products produced by their competitors. Imagine, if you will, that every time Ford produced an advertisement it was of a GM car exploding somewhere on the highway or perhaps being struck by lightening and just simply going up in air. Or, imagine if there was a very serious exposé by a Toyota spokesman listing all of the various environmental and safety defects of the latest Honda product. And imagine that billions of dollars over a period of years was what these campaigns were all about. I suspect that even in these wide-open spaces we would all be riding bicycles across Canada, and certainly our collective faith in the automobile industry would be seriously challenged.

So my first point to you is this: if politics is held in disrespect, which it is, the first people to whom we have to attribute some responsibility for this fact are the politicians themselves. No, I don't mean this in the sense that the profession has somehow failed us or people involved in it are corrupt. Quite the opposite. From my experience that is not the case,

But there has developed a culture of negativity within the profession itself, in which it is almost impossible for us to imagine voting *for* someone or something, and in which we are always being asked to vote *against* something: "Stop this hidden agenda! Throw the rascals out!" It is absolutely endemic in the way in which the political parties approach us as Canadians. The inevitable result, and it *is* inevitable, is that more and more of us simply stop listening. We tune out. We no longer watch, we don't vote. The numbers of people voting has declined.

Politicians decry the citizenry for their lack of participation. How preposterous! We should surely challenge the politicians and say: "Give us something to vote for; tell us something good about yourself. Show us something in your leadership and vision which is compelling in and of itself. Just for a moment start your sentence by saying 'my opponent is an honourable person; my opponent makes a good product, it's just that I think my product is better.' " Imagine if, in any other walk of life, people described their competitors in business as – and these were all words used in the course of the last campaign – criminals, charlatans, medicine men, hypocrites, liars, and cockroaches. Now these are all *actual* words that I heard used by people I normally respect about their opponents! I heard this as an ordinary citizen, just watching this thing. I was absolutely appalled.

The first reason we think of politics as a nasty business made up of nasty people is because this is what politicians tell us about themselves. If only they started from a different premise: that honourable people can have legitimate differences of opinion; that there should be a presumption that conduct is not corrupt but is motivated by a genuine desire to serve the public good; that real corruption is the common enemy of everyone in public life and is, in Canada, relatively rare; and that parties do not have a hidden agenda but rather a program that can be openly debated.

I think all these statements are true. I think you all know my political background – and I don't think the Canadian Alliance has a hidden agenda. I think they have a very open agenda; I don't happen to agree with it, but I don't think it is hidden. There is nothing hidden about it. It is pretty out in the open from what I can see. I don't agree with it but it's there. I don't think the Prime Minister of Canada deserves to be called a criminal. I don't believe that for an instant. I think he is a very fine, honourable (if combative and very determined) individual for whom I have only the greatest of personal respect. I don't agree with his entire political program.

It seems to me that simple civility that we expect from our children, that we expect from ourselves when we meet each other on the street, is not too much to demand of our political leadership. Something has gone very wrong in our political culture when wild exaggeration and out-landish claims have become as endemic as violence in hockey. With the same result: the public turns off.

It is also a very different public than you might think. (Now I am entering into very dangerous territory because I come here to Calgary and make these very simple points). I don't think there is a huge gap that I have observed in travelling across the country over the last thirty or forty years. I don't believe there is a huge gap between West and East. I don't think that East is East and West is West and never the twain shall meet. I don't believe that for an instant. I believe that the values of Canadians all across the country are, increasingly, widely shared.

And I would make one other observation: people no longer have the same traditional allegiance to political par-ties that they once had. Ron Ghitter[3] very nicely introduced me, saying that "people are going to be polite to you but they will never vote for you." To tell you a true story: when I was elected in 1990 in Ontario, this was not part of the people of Ontario's life script. I mean nobody thought this was going to happen. It was not supposed to happen. It's almost like a million chimpanzees sit down and type and one day they produce *A Midsummer Night's Dream*. You know the people of Ontario keep throwing the government out, and one day they are going to throw these NDPers in.

3. Reference here is to Ron Ghitter, Q.C. Former Alberta MLA and Member of the Canadian Senate, Ghitter was Master of Ceremonies and Chair of the Chumir Foundation's inaugural event.

I went to close up my cottage, in a part of Ontario which is very conservative. There were Alliance signs all along the highway as I was driving up the other day. I went into the corner store, where I have been going since I was five years old as a kid, and the owner of the corner store who is a very, very good friend of mine said: "Bob, when you won the election it was as if Portland [the name of the village of 400 people] won the Stanley Cup. We were all up cheering." And then he looked at me and said: "But don't think for a moment that any of us here actually voted for you."

I say that only to remind all of you here that yes, there are divisions between urban and rural voters across the country. And there are divisions between Canadians who have certain different perspectives on a number of different issues, but they are by no means confined to one part of the country or the other. And it is a very serious mistake – in fact, it is a complete misconstruction of Canadian life – to try to put politics into that kind of perspective.

The other point that I want to make is that I think Albertans in particular should take some considerable pride in the way in which you and others who think like you have been able to change the political agenda in the country over the last 25 to 30 years. I think that it is a remarkable achievement. I know that there are many people who prefer to stay on the outside than to take credit for what has taken place, but just for a moment reflect on how the political agenda in the whole country has shifted and has changed. The whole premise with respect to the need for tax reform; the whole understanding of the importance of government frugality and intelligence, which Sheldon spoke about very intelligently at a time, let me remind you, when Alberta (may I even mention it here?) had a substantial deficit because of the very nature of recession in the province of Alberta. Sheldon was talking about how money should not be wasted on certain programs and how people have to refocus their energies. These are now accepted, and in good measure they are accepted because of the way in which the Western (and particularly the Albertan) experience has been widely accepted in the rest of the country.

So the notion somehow that there is a political experience underway here which is unknown in the rest of the country is just preposterous, and it creates a sense of gap or division or difference which really shouldn't be there. There *are* differences in the country. To some extent they are regional. But the regional differences have been, in my view, overblown.

There are substantial differences between urban and rural voters. Those are true in Ontario as they are in the rest of the country. I can assure you that when our party became a provincial party, all of a sudden we had debates about issues which had never been debated in the party before. Why? Because we had become a province-wide party, and all of a sudden we were representative of the broader concern. We had become as much of a rural party as we were an urban party, which was a dramatic transformation for us. And I think that has its parallel in every part of the country. I defend politics because I think it is inevitable. If we don't take responsibility for our politics there are others who will fill the gap because I think the choices we face as Canadians are important. I believe that partisanship is necessary, but I don't think it should preclude us from understanding something very crucial in life. And this is really where I want to close.

The key to learning how to live a truly mature life is found, I believe, in the famous three questions of the Rabbi Hillel.

The first question is, **"If I am not for myself, then who is for me?"** Self-interest is important. It's important to stand up for yourself. It's important to know who you are, to believe in your values. To have the courage to put forward your identity. To stand up and fight for yourself.

But Rabbi Hillel's second question is, **"If I am only for myself, then what am I?"** The key experience in becoming a human being is learning that there are other people and that other people are not extensions of ourselves. Most of us in our lives learn this and I think that one of the reasons that Sheldon believed so strongly in public education is because he knew that the sooner you can learn this lesson the better off you are. If we segregate our kids too early in life they don't learn enough about "the other," so let's have them learn about "the other" right away.

We have to understand that in Canada we have become a United Nations. We have become a truly multi-racial, multi-cultural country. Now, we were from the beginning; but we haven't always appreciated it. And if you look at the most difficult problems in the world today (and I would suggest the most difficult problems we have in Canada today), they are not economic. They aren't. They are about our ability to live with one another. Think of the destruction during the twentieth century, the most destructive century in the history of the world. The violence, the people that have been killed, the people that are being killed today! Why are they being killed? Because someone else considers them to be "other," less than human, less than themselves.

Now we don't do that in Canada. We don't go to that length. But think about it with the kind of sensitivity, with the kind of attention and focus that Sheldon would have wanted you to use. Reflect on what are the greatest problems. How are we going to live together as Canadians? It's this constant tendency we have to think of our little platoon, to think that the world that we live in is the only world that counts, and that there are no other worlds. That is the kind of thinking that we cannot afford as Canadians.

We constantly have to reach out and go across and that's why the creation of national institutions is so important.  That's why the act of politics is so important because it compels us, it forces us to come out of ourselves and forces us to learn that there are other people – that people have different values.

And Hillel's third question was, **"If not now, when?"** This is where I come back to the question of leadership.

There are two things that leadership is not.  We have at one extreme prophecy, and, at the other, we have management.  There are many people who confuse leadership with these two things.

Leadership is not prophecy, because leadership requires followers – and a great many prophets do not have followers.   (Someone who was once very active in Canadian political life suggested to me that he knew he was doing well because of how unpopular he was!)  I am no longer a leader, and I don't mind saying that.  At least within my own party I am no longer a leader, and sometimes I regret that.  One of the reasons was because my followers were a little too far behind.  So if you become a little bit too prophetic (and I didn't say pathetic, I said prophetic!), you lose your way.  And you are not a success as a leader.

On the other hand there are too many people who think that leadership is management.  Management *is* important.  And the greatest of leaders are also very good managers.  Some of you may have heard the interview that I did last weekend and one of the questions on the interview was from some pollster.  (A plague on those pollsters.  Go home!  Leave us alone!  Keep your numbers to yourselves for the next twenty years; we will all be better off).  What the pollster said was that what the country is really looking for is management – good *management*.  And I said: "I don't think that is true.  I don't think the country is looking for good management. I think that what the country is looking for, what people are always looking for is leadership. They want vision." We want vision. We want someone to tell us where to go. We want someone to tell us how he or she thinks we are going to get there. We want someone who has got the courage to stand up and say: "Here are my values. I don't need to put my finger in my mouth and see which way the wind is blowing. I am going to tell you what I think the values are and I understand that leadership is not about counting heads, it's about turning heads."

And I think that's what politics at its best is all about. If I may make one brief editorial comment – that's what we missed in the last election. What we were yearning for; what we are still yearning for as Canadians, is someone telling us: "This is where I want to go. My opponents are very fine people. I would like them to come with me. I would like them to work with me. They are very fine, intelligent, upstanding people. I don't agree with all their positions. There are some inadequacies in their positions. But I don't want to talk about them, I want to talk about where I want to go and I want to persuade you to come with me." I think Canadians were looking for that. And I think that is what politics can be. I think that is what it should be. And if we decide that's what we want to make it, that's what it will be.

I just want to make one final comment before sitting down, and that is to say that Sheldon Chumir is very lucky to have had you as his friends, and, if I may say so, as his followers. Because there are very few political people in Canada today who, ten years after their death, would bring together a group of 250 people to celebrate their memory and talk about what that was all about and why that's important. I think this is a truly remarkable tribute – to him, obviously, but it is a tribute to you as well, and it's a tribute to your commitment to the kind of ideas and ideals that motivated Sheldon Chumir.

I would hate you to think that those ideals are Calgary ideals or Albertan ideals or even just Canadian ideals. I think Sheldon would have wanted them to be seen as ideals that were important around the world, important for all people, all human beings. Because there are, I think, some truths and some values that are universal. And if anybody had the courage, in Canada, to express them, it was Sheldon Chumir.

So let me thank you once again for this opportunity to be with you tonight. It's been a great chance for me to meet many of you and to share some thoughts and ideas with you. I don't always get the opportunity to speak with this many people at one time and if I have gone on a little long I hope you'll appreciate that while I am recovering, I am not totally recovered! I appreciate this chance and the time to share thoughts with you, and I wish you the very best. And once again I urge you to keep going, keep going down that path – because it is a path that is worthy of all of our best efforts.

Thank you very much.

· 5 ·

## Lindsay Gluck

# AFTERWORD:
## Civic Engagement in a Democratic Society

---

O ver the past number of years there has been much discussion of, and concern about, the general malaise
with which Canadians have been approaching traditional
party politics and civic involvement. Many authors have
noted a growing lack of engagement, especially in the
younger generation and among the many citizens who
identify with the anti-globalization movement.

This lack of engagement is cause for great concern.
Taken to its extreme, a continuing lack of interest might
altogether preclude citizens' effective engagement with the
political system. While this may be interpreted as merely
the indifference of youth, something that will evolve with
maturity, Michael Adams suggests a worrying possibility:
that young Canadians' tendency to avoid "ordinary" politics
may not be just a passing phase, but rather a fundamental
orientation that they will carry through life.[1] Adams' concern is supported by evidence that people's motivation to

1. Adams, M. "The Revolt of the Voting Classes." Environics Research Group.
(2000). <http://erg.environics.net>.

be public-spirited is developed mainly during youth, and not throughout adulthood.[2]

While it is true that participation in party politics is not the only way of engaging in society, it is nonetheless important that people should feel they have a role to play in the traditional political system. Without this key form of civic engagement, there is no guarantee that citizens will be heard by the state, let alone taken seriously. And, even more importantly, the increasingly widespread sense of disconnection from democratic structures has been shown to impoverish lives and communities.[3]

There are several theories about the relationship between a citizenry's propensity for civic association and its ability to make democracy work. As far back as 1835, social scientist Alexis de Tocqueville's great work <u>Democracy in America</u> praised the Americans for their extraordinarily successful democracy, which seemed to be based on universal and energetic civic engagement.

The association between civic engagement and a well-functioning democratic system has been recognized ever since. These days, Robert Putnam, Professor of Public Policy at Harvard, echoes de Tocqueville, theorizing that a strong and active civil society is crucial to the consolidation of democracy, because its features facilitate coordination and cooperation, and bring mutual benefits for community members.[4] According to Putnam, a community's level of civic engagement significantly influences both the quality of its members' public life, and the performance of community institutions.

The means by which civic engagement and social connectedness produce beneficial results (such as better schools, lower levels of poverty, and economic growth) are complex. Putnam suggests that something called social capital is responsible. The term "social capital" refers to abstract features of social organization, such as networks, norms, and social trust. These components of social

2. Jones, F. "Canadian Social Trends." <u>Statistics Canada Report</u> 57. (Summer 2000).
3. Putnam, R. <u>Bowling Alone</u>. New York: Touchstone, 2000.
4. *Ibid.*

organization increase community cooperation, and are advantageous for all citizens. For instance, social capital encourages communication and cooperation within social and community groups, and provides the impetus for co-operative action that reflects community members' concerns and beliefs. Putnam explains that when networks succeed in improving collective and individual civic engagement, this boosts social capital and encourages future community-minded action.

Once we recognize the importance of social connectedness and civic engagement in an effective and efficient democracy, one clear problem comes to the surface: the frighteningly obvious decline in independent civic engagement, which has now reached a point that many would describe as widespread passive reliance on the state. Citizens' growing mistrust of democratic processes and of modern politics clearly constitute a decrease in social capital. It is crucial that this be addressed if we are to ensure the continuation of a well-functioning democracy. Indeed according to Putnam, "nowhere is the need to restore connectedness, trust, and civic engagement clearer than in the now often empty public forums of our democracy."[5]

Citizens' rejection of the political process, and of civic engagement more generally, is most starkly obvious in the consistently declining voter turnout at elections. Over the past two decades, fewer and fewer Canadians have been exercising their most basic right to engage politically: their right to vote in elections. In fact, the percentage of registered voters who have voted in federal elections has dropped steadily, from 76% in 1984 to 63% in 2000.[6] Studies also show that attendance at public meetings and political rallies has fallen.

In addition to documenting behaviour that reflects a lack of political engagement, research has shown that citizens feel increasingly psychologically disconnected from

5. Putnam, 412.
6. President of the Treasury Board of Canada. "Managing for Results 2000," at Ch. 4. Tabled February 1, 2001.

politics and government than previously. There is a distinct air of mistrust toward politicians and community leaders, and a severe cynicism within communities and amongst individuals. In 1992, a Gallup poll reported that fewer that one in ten Canadians had a great deal of respect for and confidence in political parties. In the same poll, only 11% of Canadians rated MPs' honesty and ethical standards as "very high" or "high."[7] Only car dealers were trusted less than politicians![8]

Canadians' malaise toward politics is also manifested in existing political parties' inability to attract new members. As political parties attempt to reach out to new voters, it becomes clear that young Canadians are, as a group, less committed to being involved in party politics than previous generations of voters. According to MacKinnon, for instance, "The [NDP] would love to reach out to the leftist young people who have led the fight against corporate-driven globalization... but many of the movement's leaders see the NDP and Parliament as archaic instruments that are ill-equipped to fight for the cause."[9]

So what has changed? What has led to this malaise, and to the sentiment that traditional politics are not as effective as they used to be?

Some theories suggest that public mistrust of politics and government is a factor of recent historical development. The 1960s were a period of economic growth in which citizens saw the expansion of the welfare state, and benefited from greater disposable income and political stability. The next decade, the 1970s, was plagued by social and economic problems that political leaders were unable to solve.[10] Now, after relentless growth in the 1980s and 1990s, many countries (including Canada) have had to consider digging themselves out of debts that have resulted from ambitious government programs.[11] The inability of

7. Marquis, P. "Referendums in Canada: The Effect of Populist Decision-Making on Representative Democracy." (1983). <http://www.parl.gc.ca>.
8. Zussman, D. "Confidence in Public Institutions: Restoring Pride to Politics." Public Policy Forum. (2001) <http://www.ppforum.com>.
9. MacKinnon, M. "NDP A Cause in Need of A Rebel." The Globe and Mail. (March 19, 2001).
10. Marquis, *supra* 6.
11. Zussman, *supra* 7.

states to maintain financial stability has contributed to citizens' cynicism about government and politics, and to an increasingly drastic lack of political participation.

There is no doubt that globalization has changed the way we think about government. Many new forces have challenged the power of political states; in particular, giant non-governmental entities such as transnational corporations diminish the relative weight of governments. Fifty-one of the world's one hundred largest economies are now corporations rather than countries.[12] As countries' economic power is dwarfed by that of multinational corporations, governments come under increasing pressure to prove their relevance.

This shift (from a balance of power between government and big business to a situation where many corporations have become more economically powerful) has surely contributed to citizens' scepticism about government's ability to do its job. Globalization has rendered traditional governmental approaches less and less effective; governments are now struggling to redefine their roles in this new context.

Naomi Klein addresses the topic of disproportionate corporate power in her book <u>No Logo</u>. She shows that there has been a surrender of culture and education to marketing; from "cool-hunters" infiltrating the basketball courts of America's poorest neighbourhoods to efficiently mass market the "ghetto cool" style, to the surrender of schools to corporate access in order to obtain the funding required to stay up to date with modern technology, corporate power has invaded our intellectual space.

Klein also examines how mergers, synergy and corporate censorship have betrayed multi-national corporations' advertised promises of increased choice, interactivity and freedom. In this vein, she quotes an email from a Harvard Law School Fellow to Bill Gates: "If the whole idea of this revolution is to empower people, Bill, why are you

---

12. Anderson, S. and J. Cavanagh. "Top 200; The Rise of Corporate Global Power." <u>Institute for Policy Studies</u>, (December 2000). <http://ips-dc.org>.

locking up the market and restricting choices?"[13]

Finally, Klein shows that these corporations have created tenuous working environments for their employees. Corporations, she argues, have been improving the economy – but in a manner based upon job debasement and job loss. In the past, employers took on a more paternalistic role with their employees, and a person could work for the same company for decades.    Now globalization has brought deregulation and increased competition and, concurrently, lifelong careers have become a thing of the past.[14]

Despite corporations' increasing economic weight, Klein points out, the percentage of people employed within large corporations has *decreased* relative to their wealth. During a period when the world's 100 largest corporations increased their assets by 288%, the rate of growth for employment within those companies was a mere 9%.   Klein states: "soaring profits and growth rates, as well as the mind-boggling salaries and bonuses that CEOs of large corporations pay themselves, have radically changed the conditions under which workers originally came to accept lower wages and diminished security, leaving many feeling that they've been had."[15]

Overall, Klein feels that the patterns of corporate power have assaulted the social pillars of employment, civil liberties and civic space. All this has happened under laissez-faire governments like Ronald Reagan's, which in 1983 began dismantling the U.S. anti-trust laws that might have kept corporate power in check.   The erosion of governmental power has undoubtedly contributed to citizens' scepticism toward governments' ability to have a meaningful impact on their lives.

As more people recognize the impact of the new world economy, citizens' outrage has begun to fuel the next big political movement.   The inroads that private corporations have made into citizens' lives have caused many frus-

---

13. Klein, N. "No Logo: Taking Aim at the Brand Bullies." Toronto: Random House, 2000. 164.
14. Zussman, *supra* 7.
15. *Ibid.*

trated people to leave behind traditional governmental processes and to attempt a direct attack on big business. The political activists to whom the new political movement can be attributed are those same citizens who see the governmental process as archaic and ineffective. Their system is one of underground activity, information, planning and protest – not one that works toward the goal of gaining political control in a traditional sense.

Ironically, the trend in left-leaning activism directed toward corporations (including ad-busting, reclaiming the streets, and protesting) has enfeebled left-wing politics. The new generation of activists, and the anti-globalization movement, have decided that the fight must be fought outside conventional political structures. Many have adopted the view that the battle lines have been re-defined; there is a sense that it is futile to work through the traditional modes of parliamentary politics, because governments' ability to change or control what goes on in Canada has decreased so dramatically. This attitude is succinctly reflected in Globe and Mail reporter Heather Scoffield's suggestion that government no longer holds the upper hand in making sure that corporate interests do not predominate over the interests of society as a whole.[16]

The emergence of increasingly innovative technology has combined with the new political trends discussed above to put party politics in an especially precarious position. Faster, higher-capacity communication networks make it easier for citizens to mobilize for very dramatic challenges to government. For instance, the many protests that have captured the world's attention at gatherings such as the Summit of the Americas and the meeting of the World Trade Organization in Seattle would not have been as well-organized, nor would they have gathered as much support, without the internet and other communication networks.

---

16. Scoffield, H. "Untitled Speech." Canadian Business Ethics Forum, sponsored by the FGL Society, Calgary, Alberta, March, 2001.

Technology has also increased Canadians' scepticism about the government's ability to protect them from the dangers associated with rapid technological change. The increasing ubiquity of information technology has exponentially increased citizens' fear that private information will become public. The explosion of information technology has created a new responsibility for government: it must now strike a balance between the public's right to have access to information, and each citizen's right to a reasonable degree of privacy. Government must take control of this issue so that Canadians feel that they are being protected.

As the public has lost confidence in their governments' effectiveness, and that of traditional politics in general, citizens' sense of individualism has increased. Zussman suggests that as governments cut public spending on programs such as health care and education that contribute to the quality of citizens' lives, "people are electing to take care of their own interests because they do not believe that anyone else will."[17]

This increased individualism and greater focus on autonomy is reflected in the introduction of the Canadian Charter of Rights and Freedoms, which empowers individuals by outlining their individual rights and allowing them to fight for their rights in court, often at the expense of Parliament and governments.[18] It is possible that Charter challenges have undermined government's legitimacy, but more likely that they have simply exhibited our need to redefine government in changing times.

In response to increasing individualism and declining trust in governmental processes, it has become clear that politicians have certain obligations, and the democratic process must meet certain requirements, if citizens are to be engaged. In a talk about encouraging Canadians to be politically involved, Jocelyne Bourgon, former Clerk of the Privy Council, suggests that, "the relationship between gov-

17. Zussman, *supra* 7.
18. *Ibid.*

ernment and citizens can be viewed as a continuum, one which begins with transparency through information-sharing, to accountability in the reporting of results and consultation."[19]   There is also a governmental responsibility to allow citizen participation in defining problems, debating options and taking actions.

A study on populist decision-making by Bourgon explains that at one time, Canadian political culture was such that public attitudes toward political authority were ordered and acquiescent.   However, this attitude allowed for the accommodation of special interests, since governments and societal elites could put forward policy without interference from the Canadian public.[20]   Due to increasing levels of education in Canadian citizens, as well as an increase in access to information and the resulting demand for transparency and accountability, this type of political atmosphere is no longer desirable in Canada.   This has resulted in a greater need for Canadians to remain informed and engaged with political culture.  Steps must be taken to ensure that meaningful participation is not merely permitted, but also encouraged.

The importance of governments ensuring that their citizens are granted due process has been obvious recently in concerns that arose around the Summit of the Americas which met to discuss the Free Trade Area of the Americas.   Many citizens felt that the Canadian government failed to ensure a democratic political process when it refused until the last moment to release the details of the agreement being discussed, and when it erected a fence to exclude demonstrators and avoid the perceived disruption of citizen participation.  Similar situations have arisen all over the world: people have felt the need to communicate through protest in Washington during meetings of the World Trade Organization, in Prague at the World Bank meeting and most recently in Genoa at the G8 Summit, where an attempt at active participation and communica-

19. Bourgon, J. "A Voice for All:  Engaging Canadians for Change." Citizen Participation Centre.  (1998).  <www.policity.com>.
20. Marquis, *supra* 6.

tion ended in a fatality. Faith in the government and in parliamentary democracy will continue to erode as long as citizens feel that the government is shirking its duty to listen and to explain how citizens' values have been reflected in the political process.

In fact, it has been suggested that the current political system may not even be suitable for today's political culture, in which it is crucial that citizens have the ability to offer direct input. Some feel that the "first past the post" electoral system is inadequate to ensure that citizens' voices are represented in the discussion of important issues and that they will have the opportunity to affect decisions. One solution to this would be to offer more populist political instruments, such as referenda, to facilitate direct participation. However, since Canada's parliamentary tradition assumes that Canadians' wishes will be expressed through legislative representatives, there is a sentiment that this sort of direct democratic participation "embodies an important principle that conflicts with the theory and practice of representative government as we are familiar with in most mature parliamentary democracies."[21] On the other hand, there are many who believe that the current government is not, in any case, as representative as it once was.

There is an increasing concern that democratic institutions are out of sync with Canadians' values and interests. The Citizen's Forum on Canada's Future found that most people do not find the present political system to be representative of their needs and fundamental values.[22] Inaccessibility and perceived misrepresentation by governments is detrimental to the public's attitude toward politics.

As Peter Lougheed suggests, "our parliamentary democracy is based on the linked concepts of responsible government and representative government."[23] To be responsible, government must represent the people; likewise, a representative government is responsible for listening to, and acting upon, what the citizens need and value.

21. *Ibid.*
22. Marquis, *supra* 6.
23. Winsor, H. "Saving the Enfeebled Parliamentarian." The Globe and Mail. (April 2, 2001).

The fact that meaningful representation by politicians within traditional party politics is, for many, inaccessible, is therefore unacceptable.

There may be several reasons for Canadians' declining faith in governments' ability to reflect their values and beliefs. Often, it seems as though politicians simply toe party lines instead of listening to, and working for, what their constituents really value. In fact, surveys and opinion polls indicate that Canadians believe that their elected representatives do not represent them exclusively; rather, they believe MPs and MLAs represent a *combination* of constituency, regional, national and party interests, and in some cases fringe parties and special interest groups as well.[24]

There are also problems within governmental leadership that run parallel to some of the problems seen in corporate leadership. Like corporate executives, politicians often come across as self-serving, for example when their own salaries go up as government jobs and social programs are cut. This contributes to Canadians' resentful sentiments towards government, and to their idea that the system is there not to support its citizens, but rather to promote the ambitions of some select group.

Complaints about poor representation also focus on the move toward a more centralist style of government over the last decade. Centralist policies do not foster an active, engaged citizenry, and do not assist those who wish to have their values and ideals represented by governments. A report entitled Shaping Canada's Future Together, put together by a Special Joint Committee on a Renewed Canada, suggests that Canada's government "ought to explore ways and means to strengthen the representational and legislative capacities of individual members of Parliament."[25]

When citizens elect an official to government, they expect that their voices will be represented through that

24. Marquis, *supra* 6.
25. Special Joint Committee on a Renewed Canada. Shaping Canada's Future Together. <http://www.uni.ca/future/html

elected official. With centralization, there is concern that decisions are being made without such representation because many MP's are being overshadowed by the power of a select few within Parliament. MP's should have some freedom to speak and act in a way that represents their constituents, rather than merely moving in the direction of those with power. If the majority party makes decisions about its mandate from within the Prime Minister's Office instead of from within parliament, then even MPs from the majority party do not have a chance to express their constituents' views at all. This leaves citizens wondering whether those candidates who are members of the other parties represented in government have much opportunity to contribute at all.

The Citizen's Forum on Canada's Future notes that many Canadians have also become concerned that our parliamentary system is too partisan. The abrasive and adversarial behaviour that occurs in the House of Commons is beginning to undermine the public's confidence in parliamentary institutions, and in elected members' ability to represent their constituents' needs and concerns.[26] In fact, the Citizen's Forum suggests that the parliamentary process's decreasing popularity is one of the reasons that there has been a call to move some of the legislative power away from elected members of parliament and back into the hands of the citizens, through the use of direct representation. The concern is that when meaningful representation falls by the wayside, the system fails Canadians.

It is possible that in this age of perceived corporate takeover and increased branding, some younger citizens are choosing to shun the labels of partisan politics just as they shun other labels. If the government is perceived as a mere pawn of powerful multinational corporations, then it is hardly surprising that the "ad-busting" attitude would carry over to political parties that seem to be swept up in

26. *Ibid.*

the "corporate" approach to politics. And even if citizens aren't label-phobic in the political sphere, they tend to draw away from parties that spend much of their time arguing about who is the more terrible leader; many citizens would rather invest energy in causes that don't carry so much empty adversarial baggage. Instead of supporting parties that only partially represent them, and that have very little power against the corporate giants in any case, citizens are picking and choosing their causes and attempting to advance them in whatever ways they see as effective.

What steps can be taken to regain some of the lost enthusiasm for traditional politics? To begin with, it is crucial that the eroded trust be restored until Canadians can contribute to the political process, confident that the process has the capacity to function effectively. We need a government that is more efficient, more open and more honest.

An interesting and partially optimistic pattern has shown up in research on citizenship and participation: while confidence in public institutions has fallen consistently, interest in the institutions has not. In Canada, the proportion of citizens who claim to be 'very interested' in the work of political leaders has nearly tripled between 1981 and 1990.[27] How ironic to think that in a time of ever-declining political engagement, interest in politics has increased as never before! A more interested electorate is paying more attention to politics, and there is no reason to believe that Canadians are not interested in turning government and politics in a more positive direction. However, this is not an easy task: restoring faith in our parliamentary system for the sake of effective democracy is going to require great effort.

To initiate change, government needs to show citizens that it has the capability – and the nerve – to rein in big business. The balance of power between corporations and government needs to be recalibrated, because in an

27. Zussman, *supra* 7.

increasingly globalized world, there is a sense in which the power of governments will inevitably continue to decline.

A good example of the need to recalibrate power is in the field of media business. The Canadian Radio, Television and Telecommunications Commission was once able to regulate most of what went on in the media. But the internet – and the continual mergers between media "giants" – places some parts of the media increasingly out of reach for such regulation. For instance, a recent CRTC decision will allow journalists who work for media conglomerates CanWest Global and Bell Globemedia to work for their companies' print *and* broadcast operations. As a result, the diversity of perspectives will decrease and the duty for reporters to spread their loyalties over several conjoint corporations will increase as they report. This will scarcely improve journalistic coverage.

It is also important that government gain control over emerging technology, so that it can be used in a way that is helpful rather than harmful. As mentioned above, the potential for loss of privacy must be weighed against the potential for positive access to information, so that technology can be used to enhance our democracy and our governmental system. Removing the information barrier through the use of technology can help to enhance citizens' trust of the political system, rather than doing the opposite.[28]

The more dubious that Canadians become about government's ability to regain power, the more firmly they will focus on values of autonomy and independence. This reduces social capital and harms the democratic system.[29] Only after the government has regained control will Canadian citizens feel that, through party politics, they can have a voice in deciding what happens.

In addition, we need to see the government focus more on the world, and on Canada's relationships with other countries.[30] Then, perhaps, Canadians will begin to

28. *Ibid.*
29. Adams, *supra* 1.
30. *Ibid.*

feel a greater engagement both in the global system and in Canadian politics. Certainly, without a restored faith in governments' ability to maintain a balance of political control, Canadians and other citizens of the globe will continue to search for alternative, more autonomous ways of engaging in civil society.

In order to reshape political ideals so that they appeal more broadly to Canadians, it would also be appropriate to encourage some fundamentally important values within the government. Trust in government can be improved in two basic areas: accountability and transparency.

In order to make our institutions more legitimate, it would be helpful if they could find ways to communicate less confrontationally. In Parliament, instead of aggressive question periods in which demands for accountability have been more effective at discrediting politicians and the political process than they have been at serving their purpose of holding government to account, a new tool must be developed if we are to have good, effective government.

It is also important that the performance of government and politicians should be tracked and measured. Public institutions can be made open and accessible to citizens by using information technology; this makes it easier for citizens to remain informed. In fact, all levels of government are already working towards this. By 2004, the federal government plans to provide citizens with an electronic portal, that is, a 'single-window' for information about transactions with federal, provincial and municipal governments.[31] Since credibility is tied to accountability and transparency, the implementation of these kinds of programs can be highly useful in re-establishing Canadian confidence in the government.

Transparency is crucial if citizens are to be properly engaged in the political process, and if they are to trust the system to meet their needs. Citizens should have

31. Zussman, *supra* 7.

access to direct, unfiltered information about what their governments are doing, and about what values their governments are upholding. Information can be easily and appropriately disseminated using information technology, as long as it is provided within appropriate limits. Increased transparency will improve trust and ensure accountability.

Once we have begun to improve trust in our public institutions, it will be possible to encourage citizens to participate more regularly in the democratic process. This can be done in several ways. Instead of promoting the vote as the only possible means of civic engagement, there are many more meaningful ways in which citizens can also become involved.

For instance, citizens ought to demand ethical behaviour by politicians. If we allow politicians and the government to act unethically, the system's integrity will continue to erode. Additionally, there is potential for the creation of a system by which political candidates are selected, rather than simply casting about for people who can run for office. This way, we can ensure that appropriate people become candidates, and that all candidates have an ethical standard that exemplifies good leadership and representation. There might even be room for some sort of candidate training, in which citizens' expectations could be expressed.

By ensuring that citizens are able to take part in the political process at all levels, with increased governmental transparency and accountability, there will be a greater impetus for involvement.

And, mirroring the need for greater public involvement, parliamentarians should become more responsive to the public will. They must recognize that citizens' input and views are relevant; without compromising their own values, and the principles upon which they were elected, parliamentarians must take great pains to accommodate the public's values and beliefs. Essentially, parliamentary traditions must reflect – and be seen to reflect – the diversity of peoples and opinions that exist in our country.[32]

Todd argues that Canadians are best served through the democratic election of their representatives as long as those representatives act on behalf of voters in way that show integrity and reflect voters' interests.[33] However, if we wish to maintain our current parliamentary process without moving toward modes of more direct participation – such as referendum-made decisions – it is also crucial that we deal with allegations that MPs are hamstrung by party discipline.[34]

Each Member of Parliament must have a reasonable measure of freedom from party discipline so that he or she can work in the public interest, and have a meaningful impact on legislation.

There must be a collective effort on the part of political leaders, schools and the media to improve public perception of politics, and to promote civic participation. Relatively few Canadians today would consider politics a noble career; yet, as Greene and Shugarman note in Honest Politics: Seeking Integrity in Canadian Public Life,[35] politicians need to change their reputation until they are seen as honest and trustworthy if our democracy is to regain its strength.[36]

An overriding cynicism has developed toward the political system, simply because that system has been unable to keep up with the significant changes that have taken place in the last few decades. This cynicism could be alleviated if an effort were made to address politics and political issues in a new light.

Politicians must behave in such a way that not only do they act within the law, but they also try to meet a higher standard of behaviour. Politics will not be regarded as admirable unless its practice is considered ethical. Not only is this an attainable goal; it is an essential one.

32. Special Joint Committee on a Renewed Canada. "Shaping Canada's Future Together." <http://www.uni.ca/future.html>.33. *Ibid*.
34. Zussman, *supra* 7.
35. Ian Greene and David Shugarman. Honest Politics: Seeking Integrity in Canadian Public Life. Toronto: James Lorimer & Co.: 1997.
36. Todd, M. "Ethical Politics in Canada is both Attainable and Essential, York Authors Insist." York University Gazette 29:21. (February 24, 1999).

Some critics believe that Canada has made significant progress in conflict of interest issues with the implementation of the office of the Ethics Counsellor. The federal Ethics Counsellor has provided counselling to elected members in situations of ethical dilemma,[37] which has probably contributed to an almost complete absence of significant conflicts. The impartial guidance offered by the ethics counsellor has strengthened our democracy by encouraging a standard of behaviour that is above reproach.

The education system is also in a position to move toward a more positive attitude towards politics by developing political literacy and knowledge of civics. As mentioned above, public-mindedness is developed in youth, and if an appreciation of the role of government in our society is not developed in young people, it will surely be unattainable in adults. Encouraging young people to be active in their communities will foster a greater appreciation of the role of civic institutions. It is also important that students gain an understanding of what constitutes high-quality civic participation. Ethical values and ethical decision-making ought to be stressed; students should be taught the importance of responsibility, accountability and transparency in civics and leadership. This will provide young Canadians with the skills they need to be effective leaders and to demand ethical leadership. A more positive attitude toward civics will also make the idea of serving in parliament more appealing. If politics is considered a respectable and worthy profession, and its importance to a well functioning democracy is stressed in youth, then it will attract the best and the brightest that society has to offer.[38]

The media could also play a role in increasing both public trust in government, and public interest in civic involvement. What exists is a destructive cycle in which the media's need for an audience, and politicians' need for media attention, create a nasty atmosphere that focuses more upon the sensational and the salacious than upon

37. *Ibid.*
38. *Ibid.*

rational and civil comprehensive debate. Since three out five Canadians claim to base their political decisions on policies, there is a tendency for citizens to tune out meaningless media attention; this contributes to the air of political disenchantment.[39] However, the media are in a position to right this problem. Instead of mocking politicians and politics, journalists could engage in constructive and open-minded discussion, and could serve the public interest by providing up-to-date and accurate information in a relevant and socially responsible manner.

We need to focus on improving confidence in our public institutions in order to ensure that we do not undermine our civil society. Since the role of government is now more complex, perhaps, than it has been at any other time, we must remind ourselves that we are in a period of transition. Our efforts today will help to ensure that our democratic system survives, and that citizens' faith in government is restored.

We can look to Robert Putnam's theory of social capital to remind ourselves of the importance of being engaged citizens. As he suggests, the quality of public life rests on the capacity for members of our community to form networks of civic engagement, so that cooperation can ensure an efficiently functioning society. Individuals, community groups, legislators, and members of the public service must work *together* to create the networks that will allow for good government. We must also take advantage of new resources, particularly information technology, that can facilitate honesty and transparency in order to educate our citizens and to contribute meaningfully to the democratic process.

If there is one key point in Putnam's theory about social capital, it is that, while it may be difficult to restore public trust in government and to boost civic engagement, it is certainly worthwhile to do so. Through social connectedness and strong civic engagement, we can ensure the survival of our democratic society.

---

39. CBC Commentary. "Time to Break the Spin Cycle." <u>Environics Research Group</u>. (December 7, 2000). <http://erg.environics.net>.

## Works Cited

Adams, M. "The Revolt of the Voting Classes."
Environics Research Group. <http://erg.environics.net>.

Anderson, S., and J. Cavanagh. "Top 200; The Rise of
Corporate Global Power." Institute for Policy Studies.
(December. 2000). <http://ips-dc.org>.

Bourgon, J. "A Voice for All: Engaging Canadians for
Change." Citizen Participation Centre.
<www.policity.com>.

Canadian Constitution: Part 3, Shaping Canada's Future
Together. <http://www.uni.ca/future/html>.

CBC Commentary. "Time to Break the Spin Cycle."
Environics Research Group. (December 7, 2000).
<http://erg.environics.net>.

Jones, F. "Canadian Social Trends." Statistics Canada
Report: 57. (Summer 2000).

Greene, Ian. and Shugarman, David. Honest Politics:
Seeking Integrity in Canadian Public Life. Toronto: James
Lorimer & Co.: 1997.

Klein, N. No Logo: Taking Aim at the Brand Bullies.
Toronto: Random House, 2000. 164.

MacKinnon, M. "NDP A Cause in Need of A Rebel." The
Globe and Mail. (March 19, 2001).

Marquis, P. "Referendums in Canada: The Effect of
Populist Decision-Making on Representative Democracy".
(1983). <http://www.parl.gc.ca>.

President of the Treasury Board of Canada. "Managing for Results 2000," at  Ch. 4.  (Tabled February 1, 2001).

Putnam, R. <u>Bowling Alone</u>. New York: Touchstone, 2000.

Scoffield, H. "Untitled Speech." <u>Canadian Business Ethics Forum</u>. (2001).

Todd, M. "Ethical Politics in Canada is both Attainable and Essential." <u>York University Gazette</u>: 29:21. (February 24, 1999).

Winsor, H. "Saving the Enfeebled Parliamentarian." <u>The Globe and Mail</u>.  (April 2, 2001).

Zussman, D.  "Confidence in Public Institutions: Restoring Pride to Politics." <u>Public Policy Forum</u>. <http://www.ppforum.com>.

# CONTRIBUTORS

**Alan Borovoy, O.C., LL.D.** has been, for more than thirty years, General Counsel of the Canadian Civil Liberties Association. Often described as "Mr. Civil Liberties in Canada," Mr. Borovoy is the author of three books: *When Freedoms Collide* (1988), *Uncivil Obedience: The Tactics and Tales of a Democratic Agitator* (1991), and *The New Anti-Liberals* (1999). A long-time community organizer, he has published numerous articles on civil liberties issues, has provided testimony before Parliamentary Committees, presentations to public inquiries, has appeared on a wide range of public affairs radio and television programs, and has been a lecturer at several Canadian universities. Mr. Borovoy earned B.A. (1953) and LL.B. (1956) degrees from the University of Toronto, and holds Honorary Doctor of Laws degrees from Queen's University, York University and the University of Toronto as well as several other awards and honours. In 1982 he was named an Officer of the Order of Canada.

---

**M**aureen A. Maloney, Q.C. is Co-director of the Institute for Dispute Resolution and Professor of Law at the University of Victoria, British Columbia. She returned to the University, and to her position in the Faculty of Law, following a term as Deputy Attorney General and Deputy Minister, Ministry of Attorney General (B.C.) (1993 – 2000).

Professor Maloney, LL.B. (Warwick), LL.M. (Toronto), is a distinguished administrator and legal scholar. Before assuming her appointment with the Ministry of Attorney General in 1993, she was Dean of the Faculty of Law at the University of Victoria and President of the Canadian Council of Law Deans. She has published and lectured widely in the field of tax law, tax policy, women and the law, and aspects of the law affecting disadvantaged groups and most recently, in the human rights and administration of justice area especially in developing countries. Professor Maloney has also participated actively on professional bodies such as the Legal Education Council, NEED Crisis Centre, Lawyers for Social Responsibility, the Victoria International Development Education Association, and Chair of the Institute for Dispute Resolution. During the past few years, Professor Maloney has also been involved in justice reform and dispute resolution projects in China, South Africa and Guatemala.

Professor Maloney teaches "Dispute Resolution and International Hurnan Rights" in the interdisciplinary graduate program in dispute resolution in the Faculty of Law at the University of Victoria. She is also developing a course on the administration of justice and restorative justice.

---

**P**eter **Desbarats**, Maclean Hunter Chair of Communications Ethics at Ryerson Polytechnic University, was Dean of the Graduate School of Journalism at the University of Western Ontario in London, Ont., from 1981 until 1997. From 1995 to 1997, Professor Desbarats was on leave from Western to serve as one of three members of the Commission of Inquiry into the Deployment of Caradian Forces to Somalia. Following this, Professor Desbarats published his book *Somalia Cover-up – A Commissioner's Journal.* Educated in Montreal at Loyola College (now Concordia University), Professor Desbarats worked in London's Fleet street for Reuters news agency, in Winnipeg as the legislative reporter for *The Winnipeg Tribune,* as political reporter and foreign correspondent for *The Montreal Star* and as national affairs columnist for *The Toronto Star.* In the 1960s he hosted the CBC's supper-hour news and current affairs show in Montreal and in the 1970s was co-anchor and Ottawa Bureau Chief for Global TV, winning the 1977 ACTRA Award for best news broadcaster.

Professor Desbarats has wntten twelve books since his first, *The State of Quebec* was published in 1962. In 1976, he wrote a best-selling biography of Rene Levesque, Quebec's first separatist Premier. He is the author of a standard journalism text *Guide to Canadian News Media* and was co-editor in1998 of *Freedom of Expression and New Information Technologies* published in Montreal under UNESCO auspices to commemorate the 50th anniversary of the Declaration of Human Rights. He has lectured on media issues across Canada and to academic and lay audiences in the United States, Latin America and Africa. He is the author of three books for children, several plays, and numerous academic and popular articles. He is a regular contributor to *The Globe and Mail* and the Ottawa Citizen and writes a weeky column for *The London Free Press.*

Professor Desbarats is a Director of the Canadian Journalism Foundation and chairs its annual Excellence Award. He is also the chair of the Fouundation's Research committee. He is a Director of the Canadian Civil Liberties Association. In London, Professor Desbarats is on the board of the Lawson Museum of Archaeology, Advance London (a civic promotion group) and for many years was a member of the board of Orchestra London.

---

**H**on. **Robert Keith Rae, P.C., Q.C., LL.D.** is partner at the Canadian international law firm Goodmans. He served as Premier of Ontario frorn 1990 to 1995, and was eiected eight times to federal and provincial parliaments before his retirement from politics in 1996. He led the New Democratic Party of Ontario from 1982 to 1996, and served as Leader of the Official Opposition before becoming Premier.

Mr. Rae holds B.A. and LL.B. degrees from the University of Toronto and was a Rhodes Scholar from Ontario in 1969. He obtained a B. Phil. degree from Oxford University in 1971 and was named a Queen's Counsel in 1984. Mr. Rae received an Honorary Doctorate of Laws firom the Law Society of Upper Canada in 1998, and was appointed to Her Majesty's Privy Council for Canada in the same year. He also received an Honorary Doctorate of Laws from the University of Toronto in 1999.

Mr. Rae is the National Spokesperson of the Leukemia Research Fund, a member of the National Advisory Committee of the Canadian Bone Marrow Registry, and a member of the International Council of the Asia Society. He is also the President of the Forum of Canadian Ditchley Foundation, the Canadian Institute of Advanced Research and the Institute for Research on Public Policy. He has recently served as the Chief

Negotiator of the Canadian Red Cross Society in its restructuring, and is a member of the Security and Intelligence Review Committee for Canada.

Mr. Rae is a governor of the University of Toronto, an Adjunct Professor at the University of Toronto, an Associate Fellow of Massey College, and a trustee of the University Health Network. He is also the author of two books: *From Protest to Power* and *The Three Questions.*

---

**L**indsay Gluck was the 2000–2001 Intern with the Sheldon M. Chumir Foundation For Ethics in Leadership. As the Foundation's first Intern, Lindsay's work focused on research, program development and community outreach, including helping to organize the December symposium, planning the Foundation's first two community forums, and preparing its first two newsletters.

From 1995–2000 Lindsay, from Milton, Ontario, attended Queen's University, Kingston where she earned two degrees – a Bachelor of Science in Life Sciences and an Honours Bachelor of Arts in Philosophy. While at Queen's, Lindsay volunteered, over a four-year period, with Frontier College, a national literacy organization. As part of this program Lindsay chose to work with the Prison Literacy Initiative where she did tutoring and eventually became student chair of the program.

Lindsay is currently a student in the Faculty of Law at the University of Calgary. Her interests lie in environmental ethics, business ethics and policy development in bio-medical ethics.